THE BOSS SHOULD BE A WOMAN

To All Working Women!

You can manage your way to the top and compromise nothing.

"Jack McAllen, a retired business executive, offers you, the working woman, step-by-step directions to improve your career and job status, and bring you a happier, more fulfilling work life."

"This book clearly confirms the author as an authority on women in the workplace."

"If women would only read and apply what is written here, their lives would be enriched a thousandfold."

THE BOSS SHOULD BE A WOMAN

How to Manage Your Way to the Top and Compromise Nothing

How to Succeed BECAUSE You Are a Woman

Jack McAllen

Blue Dolphin Publishing
1993

Published by Blue Dolphin Publishing, Inc.
P.O. Box 1920, Nevada City, CA 95959
Orders: 1-800-643-0765

ISBN 0-931892-56-2

Library of Congress Cataloging-in-Publication Data

McAllen, Jack. 1929-
The boss should be a woman : how to manage your way to the top and compromise nothing : how to succeed because you are a woman / Jack McAllen
p. cm.
Includes bibliographical references.
ISBN 0-931892-56-2
1. Sex discrimination in employment. 2. Sex role in the work environment. 3. Women executives. 4. Women—Employment. 5. Career development. I. Title.
HD6060.M39 1993
650.14'082—dc20 93-28066
CIP

Printed in the United States of America by
Blue Dolphin Press, Inc., Grass Valley, California

9 8 7 6 5 4 3 2 1

Dedication

I wrote this book for all women, to guide and inspire them to overcome all obstacles that prevent them from gaining equality and improvement in the workplace.

I dedicate this work to all the women in our family and specifically to my wife, Nancy; our daughters, Ellen Marie Tepsick and Beth Veca; our daughters-in-law, Vicki McAllen and Anne McAllen; and the future aspiring women, our grandchildren, Jennifer, Amy, Amanda and Emily McAllen. My sincerest wish is that this book will inspire them to reach for a life beyond tradition, that they will challenge male dominance and that they become pacesetters and examples for others to follow.

Acknowledgments

I would like to acknowledge and thank the following women for their contributions, thoughts and ideas in preparing this book. Without their sincere, honest and candid offerings, this book would have never reached its heights of value nor would it have offered such a strong message. These women are Carla Corroto, Anne Michael-Daly, Thais Davidson, Christine Solich, Beth Veca, Eileen Morelli, Linda Shear, Diane Greggo and Ellen Marie Tepsick. I thank you all and hope the message of this book will inspire and lead you through successful and happy careers. Many, many others, too numerous to list, also contributed tremendously to this writing, and I thank them as well.

I wish to express a very deep, sincere and heartfelt "thank you" to my daughter, Ellen Marie Tepsick, whose total devotion to this project, with long, long hours of computer work and editing, insured its successful completion. She is an outstanding example of the true focus of this book. She performed this miracle in addition to teaching school, attending to the demands of mothering two boys and being a good wife to an understanding husband. We should all thank her for her labors on behalf of women.

Raise your sail one foot
and you get ten feet of wind.
—Chinese proverb

Table of Contents

Preface

Until now I have forcibly contained my emotions and restrained myself from preaching my total abhorrence toward the horrible mistreatment and insults women have suffered over the years in the workplace.

My name is Jack McAllen. I am a heterosexual man writing about women's problems with men. You may question what qualifications a man has to write this book. Let me say first that I have lived the greater part of my life working with women in supervisory and management positions. From this I have discovered that I like women and their overall attitude toward work. Furthermore, anyone who really knows me will quickly agree that I have difficulty keeping quiet when something really gets to me, especially when it's unfair. Well, something has! I can no longer accept the dishonorable and repressive way women are treated in the workplace. I will contain myself no more!

No matter what you read or hear, by whoever chooses to offer it, women are still not by any means being treated equally in the workplace, especially in the area of salary. Women continue to be on the blunt, receiving end of injustice, unfair treatment and rejection.

This book is written as a reaction to this poor treatment. It offers solutions and positive steps that women can take to overcome these indignities and injustices. This book examines many aspects of women at work, such as being mentally challenged by an inconsiderate boss or a work situation that borders on the impossible. It is designed to open up the minds of career-oriented women by virtue of building greater self-confidence, positive thinking, enthusiasm and risk-taking skills. It is the only book written for women that is as complete and detailed concerning the many contributing factors that restrict them. It is also the only book that offers such honest, direct and workable solutions to women's problems in the workplace. The directions and teachings of this book are born from observation and day-to-day working, walking and talking with some of the finest women in the world, many of whom, if given the equal opportunity that the law allows, would excel far beyond what men expect and, in many instances, far beyond their male counterparts.

The initial response to my book has been overwhelming, immediate acceptance by women. I have been additionally motivated by their exuberance and encouragement. On the other hand, the men who read the manuscript generally became quite defensive, looked for excuses and made denials of mistreatment. These men still for the most part view women from a stereotypical point of view.

After observing the disgraceful activities of our elected officials and after continually reading, week in and week out, about the fraud, deceit, theft and misrepresentation by senior corporate executives, I suggest that the time is ripe for women to get totally involved and take the lead in getting us out of this degrading, costly and embarrassing mess. This book prepares women to do just that. It encourages women to aspire to all positions that were previously "off-limits" and advises them clearly as to how to "manage their way to the top," by doing it *their* way, not the way set down traditionally by men and their "good ol' boy" networks and shenanigans.

It took a great deal of courage and audacity for me to address this subject so vehemently. Very few men would! Some said I was "nuts" to put myself in a position to be criticized by both sides. However, I have found that women are elated that someone is addressing workplace problems from a hands-on, experienced perspective, and that someone is offering workable solutions and answers to their many contemporary problems.

As you read the following chapters you will soon become convinced that I am qualified to write about these particular facets of women's mistreatment. The text is enriched with real-life situations and offers a common-sense approach. Apply what is written and you will realize immediate improvement and success in your job.

I worked for 44 years hiring, managing, mentoring and disciplining women. It was my privilege to manage and guide the aspiring careers of hundreds. In any single assignment, as many as 1,000 women at a time relied on me for training and career advancement and, over the span of my career, there were literally thousands. I know what motivates women to work hard and I know what causes them to hurt. I know also that they cry for recognition and acceptance.

Sex will not be openly discussed in this book nor will sexual harassment. Too much has already been written about these subjects. To dwell on these would confuse the main purpose of this book, which is to teach, solve problems and produce answers and directions.

I am not a feminist nor part of any movement. What you read is not a new version of yesterday's anything. It is not just another outdated approach, criticism, worn-out discussion or "good ol' men" bashing. Oh, I bash a few men—but only those who need it. I am ruthless with any man who joyfully mistreats, misuses and oppresses any woman who is trying to get ahead or just perform her job. I openly attack men who purposely hold back a bright, well-educated, aggressive woman simply because she is a woman.

With the new focus on women and their gaining of equality as we approach the 21st century, it is interesting to observe the parade of concessions being offered to them in terms of political appointments, the "Year of the Woman" celebration and continual improvements of their image by the press. Women are "on a roll," so to speak. While such events are generally understood as being positive for women, I just can't help but warn them of the false and token offerings that much of this media blitz represents. Much of it consists merely of surface appeasement and insubstantial acclamations. No real redemption lies in all this attention and my guess is that, as soon as the media pressures subside, the good treatment will too. Sorry for the cynicism, but the evidence already exists.

On the other hand, some of what has been offered to women has been real and honest, and all women who have achieved top status in their careers must be acknowledged for their successes. However, for the masses of women in the general workplace, we are still waiting for proof of sincerity and equality at all levels of employment.

WARNING! Some men might get upset or feel put upon if they read this book. I ask them not to lose control, but calmly to apply the age old rule that, "If the shoe fits, wear it," and to take a good, long, hard, honest look at themselves.

My record of working with and respecting women will stand *any* test, and I am proud of it. My opinions and ideas are offered honestly, sincerely and with the hope that they will be read and applied to a profitable end. You will find my intentions honorable and my motives quite clear.

If you read and apply these ideas, theories and learned experiences, you will immediately begin to succeed in your daily assignments and in the way you approach your boss and others in authority. You will learn how "the system" works, how to make your moves in order to dance around "their" games and how to position yourself more competitively. You will learn all of this proficiently because you are a woman!

I guarantee that you will find this book a positive source of strength and self-confidence, and you will learn to apply its teachings in a woman's way—not *his* way. You need this book because it is a great tool to increase your success and happiness. It was written for you by a man who really cares about your personal growth and happiness.

Nothing is particularly hard
if you divide it into small jobs.
—Henry Ford

Introduction

The focus of this book is to motivate and inspire women of all working ages to reach out for the jobs, careers and incomes that were previously off limits. It aims to guide and empower women with career tools that help destroy the outrageous and pitiful treatment they have endured for years. By emphasizing self-confidence, risk-taking, perseverance and enthusiasm, it targets the contemporary workplace where management and supervision continue, in most instances, to disqualify women's accomplishments and progress simply because of gender. This book offers guidance and solutions to overcome structured roadblocks, and it instructs how to deal with persons who continue to practice the repression of women.

Much time, extensive research and the vast experiences of the author have gone into the writing of this book, and it has become an outstanding self-training tool for women to study and follow. It wasn't written on a whim or a dare but because of the need to help elevate women to equal positions in the workplace and eliminate that subjective title of "minority" once and for all. The examples of mistreatment contained herein are drawn from the lives of real women—most of whom I know personally—and others who stand out as distinguished examples. Their names are protected by omission so they will not experience further hurt as a consequence of disclosing their hurtful and degrading experiences in an effort to help others. Fair treatment and fair play are what this effort seeks and what women crave. Just give women an equal chance—then get out of their way!

We really need women today. We need them in roles that enable them to use their instincts, intellects, thoughts and ideas in government, business or any leadership position. They can offer a splendidly different approach—*one of quality*. Society can no longer refuse them admittance to the boardrooms of companies, to high level positions in government including the presidency, and to other critical areas, such as leading roles in criminal justice, university professorships, presidencies or any high- or medium-level position.

Society needs women's input. *We need you and we need you now*—is my appeal. It is time for you to prepare and train for such leadership positions and seek to improve your status in your personal career, in this country and throughout the world. This book is designed to help you do this—your way, not his—and without compromise.

I urge you—NO! I *plead* with you to accept all new challenges and prove your worth. Prove how capable you really are. Help lead the country, its businesses and its spirit to new heights, and you will indeed help all womanhood gain her rightful position as men's equal.

Let this book serve as your inspiration and motivation toward these goals. As the author of *The Boss Should Be a Woman,* I know you will succeed.

Once made equal to men,
women become superior.
—Charles I, King of England

Sketch by Don Ferguson

"Do you want to speak to the 'man in charge' or to the women who really know what's going on?"

The time is now for you to prepare, educate and become involved for your own sake. There is no question of your ability, intelligence, strength or ultimate success. All that is required is for you to accept the challenge, make the commitment, trigger your ambitions and impel yourself into action.

—Jack McAllen

1

We Need You Now—The Time Is Ripe

We need women now; the time is ripe. We need to adopt women's ways, accept their unique intelligence and embrace their physical and mental strengths. I call upon you—a woman—to adjust your thinking, your past training and your own attitudes about who you are and what you should or should not be permitted to do with your life. I urge you to change your self-portrait from one of a second-class, manipulated citizen to one of an independent, free-thinking spirit who is ready to challenge all comers for your rightful place in life. It is time for you to become a standard-bearer, mentor, innovator, pacesetter and role model.

This need is urgent in all phases of government and business throughout the United States and the world. Just think of the high-profile jobs held by men, such as my favorite—their sanctuary of national political eminence. What a travesty these men have made of our esteemed form of government! Instead of having the option of excellent representation, we are forced to choose between the rich men, the richer ones and those striving to become rich by whatever means (the check scandal, the savings and loan scandal, and so on *ad nauseum*). These men are gambling with our nation's serious business. They are so entrenched in personal gain that they could care less about the consequences of their actions. When a scandal or national embarrassment hits the media, they gloss it over by saying, "In a week it won't be an issue—in a month, forgotten!" Just how arrogant can they get? They use this same arrogance in not accepting women as equals.

Another serious problem at all levels of government and in companies throughout the U.S. consists of pathological procrastination, indecisiveness and no sense of urgency. Because of Congress's vacillation in the decision-making process, a humiliating number of bankruptcy filings occurred in the late 1980s and now in the 1990s. This has caused American workers to be ridiculed, American products to be ostracized, and companies to move elsewhere in the world marketplace.

Furthermore, while we desperately need the leadership of women, a battery of excuses stands in their way, excuses that preserve and serve the privileged need of the men in power in politics—and secret, unwritten and conceptually illegal rules that companies use to impede women's progress and to keep them weak and subservient.

These secret rules and excuses generally originate from the one with the most power, the one who really doesn't want women around or too close to him. So he creates and passes down his thinking to lower levels of management, who in turn perpetuate those rules, even though they may not be based on fact. Some of these rules could be:

1. We can't promote her; she has a problem delegating.
2. If she gets pregnant, we will have to replace her.
3. We can't make her a manager; she isn't forceful enough. People will walk all over her.
4. She has only achieved some of her goals, so we will have to let her go.
5. She is too soft on employees, too much on their side.
6. If she gets married, she won't want to move. We must have everyone mobile.
7. She speaks out too much about existing, uncorrected problems. She'll have to go.
8. Men don't understand her and don't want to work with her.
9. She doesn't think like we do and it's confusing.
10. If we promote her, then we will all have to change our ways.

All of these examples and hundreds like them are being used every day to stymie women's progress. They are unwritten, and I consider them secret and, in most instances, in violation of all or some of the civil rights laws of this country. They certainly violate the woman.

A New Coalescence

Now is the time for women's equality in Congress and at all other government and corporate decision-making levels. With men, we get rhetoric, more problems and no answers—but lots of excuses. I am convinced that we need women's realistic, common-sense approach to the needs of modern America. With the current, male-dominated workplace our country receives severe criticism for its poor standards. A complete upgrading is needed, and my experience proves that women do not accept low standards when they are the decision-makers. They just do not accept poor-quality thinking and performances.

We need a new coalescence, one based on grass-roots reality, one designed to produce a firm commitment to respond to society's needs and to improve our nation's standards.

Women, you will need to make this change happen for yourselves. You will need to formulate *new rules,* new standards, that you must in turn implement, enforce and uphold. The new standards must include the premise that sexual differences must be accepted as merely physical and not permitted to preempt your ability to excel in the workplace. You must aim at excellence: you will have to become exceptional in the areas of education, experience and leadership, so that men will see your true value and be eager to follow you. You will have to work harder and be more dedicated. I urge you to reach for these higher standards and teach men what "good" really means. *You* can be the catalyst. The time is now to develop yourselves and plan your goals to succeed so that this male trend can be reversed. You can do it! You really can!

Are you ready for this challenge? Have you learned to reject failure and the embitterment of criticism? Do you feel the strong desire, the urge to stand up to all short- and long-term setbacks and to accept and promote diversity? Do you accept the certainty of equality and your ability to defend it? Do you actually see yourself in this role? If not, read on and absorb the following chapters—which offer more individual help and guidance—until you *can* see yourself in this role. You will need resolve and you won't succeed with self-doubt. You must be committed to success and be ready to prove to the world that you are as good as any man. Oh, how I want to see you succeed in this.

I know you are strong and the measure of any man. Daily I have observed the superior way in which you approach work projects and stick with them. My experience proves that you do this much better than men do. I, along with other clear-thinking men, would rather have *you* performing a job than a man because of the superior results and the time saved. You, likewise, know you are as good as any man. Now is your time to prove it, so prepare yourself for new opportunities.

George Bernard Shaw explains equality in a poignant way:

> "A woman is really only a man in petticoats, or, if you like, a man is a woman without petticoats."

The feminist movement did its job, and many people say it ran out of gas. Now it is time for you to move to the next step of the crusade and move forward individually. Please don't pass up any opportunities as they come your way, especially if you really want them and can succeed with them. Listen to me when I tell you, "You can do it." Let me help you.

When Opportunity Knocks

Forgive me for this harsh observation, but all too often you and I both have witnessed your hesitation or refusal to accept an earned promotion, new opportunity, new responsibility or any new, innovative challenge. You have turned down many a job advancement because you let your self-esteem, self-confidence or self-worth dictate your thinking. You have, in fact, resorted at times to stereotypical excuses that denounced yourself and your capabilities.

During my years of corporate experience, I watched a more deserving woman step aside so that a man could take the promotion or better job in her place. She offered the excuse, "He is raising a family and needs it worse than I do," but the real reason was her lack of self-confidence. This same lack of self-confidence forced another woman to refuse a potentially prestigious assignment, one that would have opened the door to a directorship in a new, permanent, in-house training department. A man got the job and became quite successful by using most of the woman's ideas.

Be prepared! When your boss or your superiors offer a promotion, they want you to accept. They wouldn't offer if they weren't convinced of your abilities and qualifications. When these important stepping stones come your way, take them, but don't rest; push for the next promotion—and the next. People and companies want you to succeed.

Similarly, I have further witnessed women stepping aside to let men steal their opportunities, their thoughts and their ideas, because they lacked the mental fortitude to challenge the man and claim what was rightfully theirs. Don't give up your hard-earned opportunities! Fight for your rights and what you have worked for. Don't step aside to the intimidating appearance and aggressive behavior of any man, especially if it is because you are a woman and you feel inadequate.

Opportunities do not come along very often, and good ones, rarely. They seldom come looking for you announced; they usually sneak in some morning around 11:00 or some late afternoon when you least expect them.

On the other hand, if you are interested in a specific opportunity and it doesn't seem to come your way, create the atmosphere for it to happen. Become innovative. Find the need for your abilities, experience, great personality and other positive qualifications and present them to your boss or even his boss. Good leaders and companies like this. It convinces them that the atmosphere in the workplace is good and that they are motivating people to want to get ahead.

More than anything, when that opportunity comes knocking, you can't say no to it, especially when your heart and spirit *want* you to say yes. Don't question your abilities or manufacture excuses to refuse—and don't look for an easier alternative, either; take the assignment.

Also, just consider that if you ignore or refuse the promotion, this career opportunity, you could make certain bosses very happy. Many would like you to refuse so that then they can promote one of their cronies—a man. Don't let any man take away your progress, and don't let any supervisor or boss prove his point about the inflexibility of career women by your failure to respond positively. When in doubt about a promotion or new assignment, be quick to take the risk. You will thank yourself tenfold later.

By an offer of promotion, your boss is actually telling you, "We need you now and your time is ripe!" Accept his offer so he can deliver a positive message to his boss. Accept his offer; do what is right for you—morally right.

A word of caution—few things devised by humans are perfect and, as good and as successful as you become, you will suffer setbacks. Don't let setbacks dictate your future career decisions. Some challenges will be nasty, maybe even insulting. Tears may flow (yours), and you will feel like packing it in and saying, "It's not worth it." But it is, and you know it is, and you also know that you can succeed if you hang in there. Keep this thought in mind, "I am needed and the time is ripe." You will constantly need this motivation as you face unanswered questions week after week, month after month, and you will need it during the times when you try to do your best and receive little or no attention.

Success doesn't come easy for anyone and for some it seems like an endless journey. Women are not immune to this feeling. Always remember, you have an added challenge because you are trying to overcome the inertia of thousands of years of repression.

Don't give up! Some men (like me) are just waiting and hoping you will succeed, and we know that we really do need you.

Spouse, Family, Love and Rewards

Now that you have decided to seize the opportunities that come your way, get ready to face your spouse, the one you love, with a message that will change both your lives. You will need his thorough understanding, acceptance and backing in any and all career moves. You must also include the family and plan to accommodate their needs. You will find it essential to ask for their understanding and help when they see you overworked and unable to offer love and attention affectionately, or when you display short temper during bouts of frustration. Emotionally-charged times will happen as you climb to the level of success you seek and deserve. Men go through this, and you will too. You must be relentless and utterly committed if you really want to accomplish this mission.

Your spouse and family will share the rewards of your new challenge and learn to accept your challenge as their goal as well. They will need to participate in the household, family tasks of caring for the children, doing domestic chores and setting good educational and social standards. With this you may need to remind them that they will share the personal rewards and the financial wealth that goes with success. Be prepared for the changes all of you will go through. Will your husband see you as a successful entrepreneur and accept you as an equal, especially if his friends or peers throw their chauvinistic criticism against him or you? This subject is most controversial and challenging to men, so be ready to be understanding, but firm. Do your homework well, and be ready to prove yourself.

On the other hand, if you are single and unattached, I believe you are free to take on this challenge alone and give it your all. Nothing is holding you back. This is ideal because you are accountable only to yourself.

If you are single but are serious about someone or engaged, you must proceed along the same path as if you were married. He must become a partner to your career and understand your desires. He must be conditioned to accept and back your career moves as if they were his own. It's a lot to ask of a man who may not be ready for this step, but he will adjust. (See Chapter 6—*Love, Marriage and a Career.)*

If you feel comfortable with all of this and believe you can succeed when opportunity calls, you must assume that you have at last reached "a level playing field" with those at the next step in power and you have a chance to play the game. With all of this firmly in place, it is time to accept the challenge and the risk—GO FOR IT—and take full advantage of your newfound opportunity. You will be the envy of all your friends and those who dream of their own success, and you will feel good about yourself.

The "glass ceiling," that invisible barrier that prevents women from entering the boardroom and becoming serious decision-makers, is slowly coming down. Now it is time for women to exchange the "glass ceiling" theory for a more distinctive reality—that of creating equitable incentive and a more honest code of promotion. That will be the true top reward of your success.

Women have got to make the world safe for men,
since men have made it so damned
unsafe for women.
—Lady Astor

SYNOPSIS

This chapter has been an impassioned plea for women to get involved in all phases of leadership in this country and around the world. The time is ripe for change because of mismanagement and its degrading results. The time is ripe for women, because men have started to accept them as equals. The time is *now* for you—each individual woman—to prepare, educate and become involved for your own sake. There is no question of your ability, intelligence, strength or ultimate success. All that is required is for you to accept the challenge, make the commitment, trigger your ambitions and impel yourself into action. Enlist the help and support of family as it applies, and set out to "make the world safe for men."

If we have come to think that the nursery and the kitchen are the natural spheres of a woman, we have done exactly as English children came to think, that a cage is the natural sphere of a parrot because they have never seen one anywhere else.
—George Bernard Shaw

When asked by an ardent American feminist about the future role of women, Winston Churchill said, "It will be the same, I trust as it has been since the days of Adam and Eve."

Old fashioned ways which no longer apply to changed conditions are a snare in which the feet of women have always become readily entangled.
—Jane Addams

2

Things Have Changed, But . . .

From the *Dallas Morning News*, as reported in the *Youngstown Vindicator,* Youngstown, Ohio, May 25, 1993, in part:

> UNITED NATIONS REPORT:
> "WOMEN EXCLUDED FROM POWER."
>
> Women make up more than half the world's population, but hold little more than 10 percent of parliamentary positions. . . .
>
> The United Nations says women are the largest "excluded group" in the world, lagging behind men in earning power, political influence, literacy and recognition as contributors to the global economy. . . .

> No country treats its women as well as it treats its men—a disappointing result after so many years of debate on gender equality, so many struggles by women and so many changes in national laws, the U.N. said in its fourth annual Human Development Report. . . .
>
> In industrial countries, according to the report, gender discrimination is evident primarily in employment and wages, with women concentrated in lower-status jobs and earning half as much as men.

From the above report it is evident that, despite the so-called progress that has been achieved during the feminist movement, the true status of women is still depressed and unequal. So, what really took place during the era of alleged progress for women? Let us examine the past one hundred years—a historic time of incomparable progress in job quality and quantity in America and of tremendous advancement in industry, agriculture, medicine and technology. These years were unparalleled for men, but ironically were years of poor progress for women.

The Women's Suffrage Movement. During the Women's Suffrage movement at the turn of the century, women's working conditions were abominable and their pay was substandard. Pay scales for women were a mere fraction of men's wages and the equity gap only grew larger as industry advances took men upward and onward to higher standards and greater challenges and rewards.

The working women of the early 20th century collateralized their household chores as they toiled in laundries, textiles, clothing and shoe factories and canneries. While their productivity was good, their overall prestige was low. They were considered temporary employees, at best. This made it possible for employers to repress them and keep them lowly paid, without benefits.

The mood of the era was, "Equal say will enable women to get equal pay and equal pay is dangerous." In other words, equal pay would encourage a woman to seek other improvements. She might just think twice about marriage and her part in it (as she does today). The men in control judged that this would be dangerous. It would put women on a 100% equal basis, and that was tantamount to admitting that a woman has equal intelligence. Neither men nor women with low self-esteem would accept this, and the vast majority of women went along accepting lower status.

Nonetheless, some women did come forward with strong courage, fortified with maximum self-confidence and a barrel-full of self-esteem to begin changing all of this. One of these, a woman named Mollie Schepps, took on a New York senator making a speech concerning the male domination of women during the suffrage campaign of 1912. Mollie, a shirtwaist worker, answered the senator:

> Yes, we want man's administration, but not the kind that looks well on paper or sounds good when you say it. Don't you gentlemen get me angry. Our minds are already made up as to what we are going to do with our vote when we get it!

This kind of fight-back attitude eventually took the unpaid housewife, mother and sometimes temporary worker, and gave her a chance to raise her self-esteem and self-confidence to continue to fight, fight, fight for better things, *i.e.*, more control over her own destiny. It was a good beginning, marked by high emotion and hard work.

Unfortunately, men continued to find ways to repel women's rights and keep them repressed. One way was to belittle housework, creating an image for women of less importance, less intelligence and less capability. When permitted to work, they were excluded from skilled labor jobs and from the opportunities to learn them. They were forced to accept atrocious working conditions, which by today's standards would be considered a form of slavery. They accepted low pay because there were no other choices.

Employers did little or nothing to improve conditions. The fact that women's jobs were so unpleasant and poorly paid forced women to prefer housework, especially since they were responsible for it anyway, after working hours. This repressed positioning of women enabled employers to treat them as marginal workers. As a result, managers were able to show greater profits and make themselves look good because their payroll costs were held low, and this reduced the cost of doing business, which made profits more acceptable to board members and stockholders.

The Rosie-the-Riveter Phenomenon. As time marched on, the opportunities for women did not change much until Adolph Hitler came along and Japan decided to flex its military muscles and attack us. The U.S. entered World War II on December 8, 1941. At this time every available able-bodied man was summoned to serve in the armed forces in one way or another. Women were summoned to work the machinery in factories and shipyards, drive trucks and heavy equipment, work road crews and all assortment of back-breaking, muscle-wrenching jobs. Their performance was superb. It was from the ranks of these women that the nickname "Rosie the Riveter" was born. Many, many women became riveters during this time of heavy demand. The nickname, however, soon became a moniker for every working woman.

As time went by, women became the unsung heroines of this war, which was the most destructive of life and property in our history. Everyone hailed these women, and people just couldn't say enough good things about their work. Many said at the time, and historians concur, that if it hadn't been for the women, we never would have won World War II.

It is ironic that, just a few short decades ago, women proved how strong they are, how durable and doable their work is and that they were (and are) just as strong physically and mentally as any man, when and if they really want to be. It also bears mentioning, for those men who think that women cannot manage a home along with a career, that women worked forty hours plus, six and seven days per week during this war and still managed to raise and discipline the children, run the household, do church work and USO volunteer work, entertain soldiers in their homes, and maintain a liveable checkbook balance. In addition, during this period children were better-disciplined, were better family members, loved more and certainly hated less than children of today.

Post-world-war syndrome. Then came the letdown. Most men returned home, became civilians again (1945-1946) and reclaimed their jobs, leaving women to once again return to second-class status. This did not set well with many women, and they complained. No one paid attention, however, and in the late 1940s and through the 1950s, working women suffered guilt and despondency as they were forced into less meaningful jobs, retail store clerking, seamstress work, teaching and other "female" jobs. Many felt guilty, because they knew they were capable of better positions but weren't permitted to have them. Better jobs would bring better pay and help their financial problems at home. They were paid a pittance compared to what they knew they were worth. Children still needed clothes, food and other necessities, not to mention all the newest gadgets, electronics and fashions, and so the internal self-worth/self-esteem plight of women became more deeply entrenched.

The Sixties: a rebirth. Women began to find new life as the 1960s exploded with a vengeance in favor of minority rights, and the new Civil Rights Act of 1964 became law. This legislation prohibited discrimination on the basis of race, color, religion, sex or natural origin by employees engaged in industry affecting commerce. The Equal Employment Opportunity Commission (EEOC) was established to serve as the authority in all complaints against non-complying employers. It became unlawful to refuse to hire or falsely discharge or otherwise discriminate against any individual with respect to "compensation, times, conditions, or privileges of employment because or race, color, religion, sex, or natural origin." Businesses were forbidden to "limit, segregate or classify their employees or applicants in any way that would deprive or tend to deprive them of employment opportunities or otherwise adversely affect their status as an employee."

Federal "affirmative action" was established to enforce employers in accepting and promoting the conditions, however extreme, to strengthen the new laws and to force improvements towards equalization in working conditions.

Despite watchdog efforts, the Civil Rights Act continues under fire even in the nineties. It is constantly challenged for many reasons by those in power. Some employers, but not enough, complied totally early on. Other employers said they were complying but were actually lying. Still others implemented the new directive only in part. Finally, there were and still are those who quietly neither accept the law nor change their practices, hoping no one will blow the whistle and challenge them.

Even though it was better than nothing at all, the Civil Rights Act of 1964, didn't have enough strength to stop such challenges. Too many loopholes existed, and it began to be a laughing-stock, especially to women. In 1991, however, an amendment to the Civil Rights Act of 1964 came into play. When it passed, it supposedly closed the loopholes that lawyers and employers had found to keep women (along with minorities) repressed. The law is now being tested as to its ability to take women to totally equal status.

The 1991 amendment is an extension of the original law and is more definitive about what actions are expected of employers. It locks employers into compliance more precisely and entails stronger punishment. The law is available to women to use when everything else fails. It is, and has proven to be, a strong equalizer for women in the workplace. Unfortunately, many women remain fearful of retaliation if they challenge an employer with the law. They are intimidated by the thought that their act of bringing a lawsuit against their employer will hinder their future possibilities of promotion, subject them to personal smear tactics, or otherwise ruin a good resume when they leave the employer.

Thus, at the close of the century, we can say that getting here wasn't easy. We can also say that we haven't yet arrived, by any means, in terms of achieving total equality. However, let us examine the statistics that *do* exist which show progress in women's status in the workplace.

The Rising Stars. A small percentage of women have risen in their careers to exemplary heights in recent years. The most significant thing about this is the fact that the possibility now exists to rise to the top of major corporations in traditional business forums, whereas twenty years ago that possibility did not exist.

Consider such individuals as Ellen Marram, who became Vice President at Nabisco in 1985 and then four years later took over as CEO; Karen Horn, who is Chairman and CEO of Bank One of Cleveland; Roseanne Decyk, Vice President of Commercial and Industrial Sales of Amoco Oil Company in Chicago; Susan Greenwood, President of Berkshire Bank in New York; Jane Evans, Vice President of West's Home and Personnel Services' Market Unit. These and other "rising stars" are highlighted in the November 1991 issue of *Working Woman* magazine.

In its "Breakthrough Generation" 15th anniversary report, *Working Woman* states that more than half of the surveyed corporate women had reached senior vice president level or higher. This is a measurable increase since 1985 and a giant leap forward since the 1970s. It shows that many women have in fact broken the "glass ceiling barrier," which creates hope for all women's future prospects.

Other positive gains have been made elsewhere by women in management. The U.S. Department of Labor's *Facts on Working Women* reports that women in management had advanced to 39.3% of managerial, executive and administrative occupations, as shown in Chart 1. While this represents only 10.8% of all employed women in those years, it does represent an increase from 6.3% in 1978.

CHART 1
Women in Executive, Administrative, and Managerial Occupations—1978, 1983, and 1988 Annual Averages
(16 years of age and over)

Year	Number (in thousands)	Women as Percent of: Total Persons in Management Occupations	Women as Percent of: Total Civilian Labor Force	Women Managers as Percent of all Employed Women
1988	5,590	39.3	45.0	10.8
1983	3,490	32.4	43.5	7.9
1978	2,495	26.5	41.7	6.3

In 1986, a survey of corporate women officers employed by Fortune 1000 organizations showed that, while none of the women surveyed had reached chairperson, vice chairperson, or president, four out of five were at the vice president level or above. This compares to only one in three in 1980.

Today women are more likely to be managers where there are already women employees at lower levels. Women comprise 61% of managers in the field of medicine, 49.2% in personnel/labor relations and 49% of administrators in education. Unfortunately, other fields of employment are still not open to women or have only token representation. Only 24% of purchasing managers are women and only 18% of administrators in protection services are women. Women only comprise 5% of construction inspectors and many other fields show only minute proportions of women.

Thus, as a result of the aggressiveness of a few courageous women, some doors have opened for you and there is promise of more progress in the future. This book will prepare you to take advantage of these new opportunities in supervisory or management careers at all levels and self-employment in any field you choose. This is your "new look of the 90s" (and beyond) and it is my sincerest wish that you join the ranks of those "rising stars" who reached out for high personal achievement and found success.

Remember, however, that only a few have actually reached that "rising star" status and you must not be misled into believing that things really have changed all that much. For most women in most jobs around the world, things haven't changed at all and change will never really be complete until all of the decisions in the workplace are made without gender bias.

Unfortunately, the most recent statistics clearly prove that not only are women *not* making much headway in the workplace, but they are in fact regressing as a whole. Even today, if a man and a woman are up for the same promotion and are equal in all fields—education, position, experience, time and input as team members, age—and even if they have solved all domestic considerations that might otherwise get in the way of career advancement, who gets the job? In 87% of the situations, the man would be the winner and only because he is a man. My own experiences reveal that the ratio is 8:1, men to women, in promotion situations. In this scenario, one must at the very least consider that the lone woman in fact got promoted because it doesn't look good for a company to avoid women entirely or for fear the government might begin to do its job and start enforcing some of the existing laws on equity.

You will find that men often praise the thought of change, but then decline to let it happen in their own domain. This is two-faced! In fact, today's man-in-command is apt to say, "Women have never had it so good," referring to women's new status and career potential. Then they will go on to complain, "What do women *want?*" The answer is *everything,* because women really want 50/50 representation.

Others in authority see a few "blips" of women's successes and quickly proclaim how women are making tremendous progress and that all is well now. At least that is what those who have the power to choose between men and women in the workplace have been overheard proclaiming.

These authority figures, of course, include employers and government officials alike, who have a self-distorted history of consistently exaggerating statistical reports and excusing or ignoring operating deficiencies, their own mistakes and their inequitable treatment of the rank and file.

If these men's opinions on women's progress are so accurate, let's examine women's answers to the following short quiz.

Question #1: If there is upward movement for women, is it equal?

Answer #1: ABSOLUTELY NOT! (Just ask any woman in the business arena.)

Question #2: Are women getting the same equal respect that men have cultivated and protected for each other over the years?

Answer #2: NOT ON YOUR LIFE! (Just ask any woman lawyer or architect if she has received equal peer respect.)

Question #3: If women are receiving promotions as reward for good performances, are these being delivered with the same measure of inducement as for men—inducement which propels them to progress further?

Answer #3: FAR FROM IT! Women seldom receive the salaries, stock options or mounds of perks that men do, and you rarely see them singled out in a complimentary way in the media, either. Women customarily receive their rewards as an afterthought at a staff meeting, at the end of the day while walking out the door, or in some other uncomplimentary way.

Question #4: Are women truly receiving the GOOD JOBS, the ones that carry the extras and special rewards?

Answer #4: Only if management is forced to promote them; if it is during a recession or downsizing—almost never.

Question #5: Women are now considered to be team members in many work environments, but are their thoughts, ideas and overall contributions to the whole being considered and then fully developed?

Answer #5: This is a major complaint of women. They say that if they get the rare chance to offer their thoughts, ideas, talents and so on, they seldom get an answer back or hear of it again.

Question #6: Are women's pay scales for the same work equal to those of their male peers?

Answer #6: Again, absolutely not, and not getting much better, either. Government statistics and those quoted in this book (which are the most recent available) clearly show unequal pay for the same work performed.

Admittedly, this quiz is very informal. But the fact is that one hears these questions often bandied about in meetings, group discussions and one-on-one conversations. Also, these questions touch the heart of the matter of equality and it has been my experience that, when asked, these questions receive a resounding "NO!" answer with extremely rare exceptions. SO, to accept tokenism and lip service that women have reached equality is unjust, ludicrous and falls under the description of misinformation.

Women have never had it so good? Ask the women who work full time but still have to come home and cook, wash, shop for groceries, taxi the children to their full social, educational, and athletic calendars, and be held accountable by society for managing a family.

Ask the women who have fallen victim in the early 1990s to major company down-sizing and court bankruptcy protection of their employers, employers who in the past raised the flag of equality to the top of the pole, but then quickly lowered it to half mast when it came to retaining women over men during cutbacks. Their excuses? Anything from bogus poor-performance appraisals to the creation of impossible rules concerning job transfers and relocations.

Ask the women who have been told that if they go on maternity leave, they can't be guaranteed a position when they return, or that they cannot be moved out of their present position because they are so good that they just cannot be replaced, or any other statement created to decoy or deflect the true issue.

Ask the extremely capable, very promotable woman who languishes for five years parked in an entry-level management position, watching job promotions go to men time after time, while the boss drums up more excuses.

Ask the woman I know of who devoted nine years to three separate management emphasis areas, with a "very good to excellent" appraisal in every category, who was considered when fifty prestige management positions opened up due to company expansion, and all fifty positions went to men, most of whom had lower qualifications.

Or how about another woman upon whom fortune smiled, who was allowed to become a territorial sales manager for a large, well-known international company. She responded with large sales increases for four years in one of the toughest markets in the U.S. She was totally committed to the company, her clients and herself—to excellence. But when the time came for promotion, her male boss gave the new position to someone from the outside—a friend, a man.

Fortunately, this woman went on to become the top sales manager for that multi-billion-dollar company for the entire country in that year, so she ended up beating the men at their own game. Ironically, this same woman, in a similar setting where she again consistently outperformed her male peers, was denied the benefit of a company-paid Masters Degree program, while the men around her received this benefit. She was refused because she was a woman, although the company tried to camouflage the reason. She resigned because of this blatant discrimination and she ought to take the case to court.

Women have never had it so good? Shame on those men who exercise their authority in such a manipulative, unfair and degrading way. Shame on those who make these unfair decisions and cost their companies either the total loss of such outstanding individuals or the suppression of their skills and potential contributions. Shame, too, on those at the top who consistently engage in such inequitable, denigrating games against women.

It is quite obvious that in situations such as the above, the men involved have a strong fear of women competitors and are aggressively protecting their hierarchy from penetration by women. What a waste of brain power, expertise, loyalty, dedication and superior performances such companies have squandered over the years.

SYNOPSIS

My experience over forty-plus years in management, added to those women interviewed and my research for this book, clearly support the conclusion that those who frequent board meetings, staff meetings and executive lounges still refuse to accept women as their equals. Unfortunately, they are still in control and able to influence the media and public opinion in a way that makes them look amicable and good, while they continue to protect their male empires.

Let's face up to facts: there is too much talk about women's progress and not enough action to make it happen. Women can't afford to become complacent or fool themselves into thinking that the inequities towards them have been solved as the century progressed. Most men don't understand what women are seeking and they ignore women's desires. Even if they state that they are going to help, all too often they do nothing in the end.

Recall the names of those "rising stars," those brilliant, persevering women mentioned earlier in the chapter who know that "some women are born leaders" and that this list continues to grow slowly every month. Look up to these and other women as role models. Here are a few more names to honor, as reported by *Business Week* magazine in their list of the 50 Top Women in Business, June 8, 1992:

Zoe E. Baird: Senior Vice President, and General Counsel, Aetna Life Insurance Co. This young woman, once summoned by President Clinton for the office of Attorney General, is party to all major policy decisions at Aetna.

Brenda Barnes: President, Pepsi Cola South, Pepsico. This young woman is the highest-ranking female executive at Pepsico.

Kay Koplovitz: C.E.O., U.S.A. Network. This is one of the leading networks, viewed by virtually every cable system in America.

Liz Powell: Director, Design Center, Sony U.S.A. At age 38, she is the first woman and first American to run graphics and industrial design for the Japanese electronics giant.

Rejoice in the fact that now women have a better chance to attain such high offices. You are just one commitment and one desire away from setting your own sights on a high-ranking position. The rest is up to you.

Just ask Janet Reno, the first female attorney general of the United States. She is indeed living proof that some women are born to lead.

Stupidity is also a tradition.
—Frank Dave

Change not the mass but change the fabric
of your own soul and your own visions,
and you change all."
—Vachel Lindsay

Men are vain, but they won't mind women working so long as they get smaller wages for the same job.
—Irvin S. Cobb

3

The Wage Gap Scandal

Deep within your soul, your spirit cries out to be equal, and yet the wage gap that has existed throughout this century and before defies that equality when it comes to the same pay for the same work. History has mistreated women, claimed them as "cheap" labor and labeled them as incapable.

Even today an equal pay standard eludes women, and great confusion clouds the subject, since everyone who has written an article or authored a book on the subject of the wage differential between the sexes seems to use a different set of figures for comparing the two. The disparity can be quite large and thus confusing. However, all of the figures, from whatever source, clearly point out that a difference in pay exists between men and women for the same job.

I choose to employ the figures from the Department of Labor Women's Bureau dated October 1990, the most recent available, to elaborate and explain this inequity that man has levied upon women.

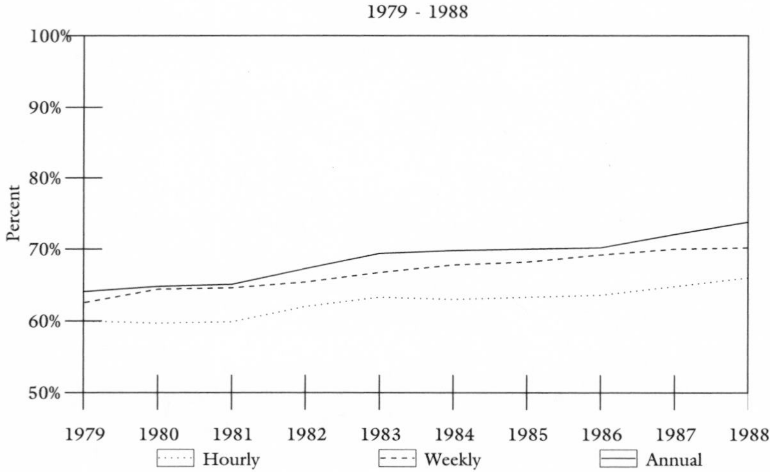

There is definitely a gap between what men and women earn for the same job. Using men's earnings as a yardstick, that is to say, showing a woman's earnings as a percentage of men's, this chart illustrates the gap, showing a small improvement from 1979 to 1988. (For reference, in the 1950s, the difference was 50%.)

In 1988, women working in the *hourly* ranks received only 74% of what men received for the same job. In the early 1990s, reports consistently show women at 70% of men's pay. Yet, for *full-time wage* and *salary workers,* women's weekly earnings were only 70% of men's annual earnings. Further, median *annual* earnings for women were only 66% of men's. This represents a shortfall comparison: women's earnings were 26% less than men's hourly earnings, 30% less for weekly earnings and a whopping 34% less for annual earnings. The three measures differ because women workers worked fewer hours than men, and those paid hourly rates are in a different group than wage and salary workers.

This government report states that all measures were from the most current Population Survey and released by the Bureau of Labor Statistics.

This, of course, is an improvement compared to the 1950s. However, at the present rate of improvement, women could *possibly* reach equality by the year 2020, which is far too long to wait.

BUREAU OF LABOR STATISTICS REPORT

Are we closing the earnings gap? Historically, we find that women's median hourly earnings as a percent of men's reported by the Bureau of Labor Statistics climbed from 64 percent to 74 percent during the decade from 1979 to 1988. Weekly earnings as reflected in Current Population Survey data show that women's earnings as a percent of men's moved from 62 percent to 70 percent from 1979 to 1988. Median annual earnings for women changed from 60 percent of men's earnings in 1979 to 66 percent in 1988.

This chart provides perspective on women's gains over the decade. We see that the direction is toward greater equality, but some find the pace extremely slow. Full equality would be 100 percent. The following table, also from the Bureau of Labor Statistics, presents the percentage ratios from which the chart was developed.

Women's Earnings as Percent of Men's

Year	Hourly	Weekly	Annual
1979	64.1	62.5	60.0
1980	64.8	64.4	59.7
1981	65.1	64.6	59.9
1982	67.3	65.4	62.0
1983	69.4	66.7	63.3
1984	69.8	67.8	63.0
1985	70.0	68.2	63.3
1986	70.2	69.2	63.6
1987	72.1	70.0	64.8
1988	73.8	70.2	66.0

An earlier history of women's wages, from the U.S. Historical Statistical Data, Appendix 1 (below), representing only a small portion of the working women of that era, again points out the low pay women received for equal or similar work.

In twenty-five manufacturing industries, the earnings hours and wages were as follows:

AVERAGE WEEKLY EARNINGS MALE	AVERAGE WEEKLY EARNINGS FEMALE
1920 - 49.2 hrs. = $31.69	43.0 hrs. = $17.71
1930 - 44.5 hrs. = $27.99	40.5 hrs. = $15.98
1940 - 39.2 hrs. = $30.64	35.5 hrs. = $17.43
1948 - 40.7 hrs. = $60.98	38.4 hrs. = $41.86

AVERAGE HOURLY RATES BY YEAR

	MALE	FEMALE
1920 -	$.64 per hour	$.41 per hour
1930 -	$.62 per hour	$.395 per hour
1940 -	$.78 per hour	$.49 per hour
1948 -	$1.50 per hour	$1.09 per hour

The wage drop illustrated in 1930 for both males and females was due to the Great Depression. Similarly, the increase in 1948 was a result of the post-war period and the beginning of the biggest growth period in American history.

Additional government reports further state that, traditionally, women have "crowded into a few occupations." In 1989, the six most prevalent occupations for women were, in order of magnitude:

1. Secretaries
2. Teachers (excluding those in colleges and universities)
3. Semi-skilled Machine Operators
4. Managers and Administrators
5. Retail/Personnel Sales Workers
6. Accounting Clerks

About one-third of working women were employed in these occupations.

In 1970, the leading occupations for women were:

1. Secretaries
2. Sales Clerks (retail)
3. Bookkeepers
4. Teachers
5. Typists
6. Waitresses
7. Sewers and Stitchers
8. Registered Nurses
9. Cashiers
10. Private Household Cleaners and Servants

Many women continue in these traditional positions today, not just because they feel comfortable there, but mostly because men keep them enclosed by tradition in order to prevent them from infiltrating into the male-dominated fields.

For those few, bright, trend-setting pioneers who have managed to establish themselves outside of tradition, the pay is still far from what the top people in their field are receiving. To illustrate this, *The Ladies Home Journal,* in an article about careers of the eighties, states the top jobs for women reveal the following wage differences:

JOB DESCRIPTION	WOMEN NATIONAL AVERAGE	MEN TOP PEOPLE
Manufacturer's Representative	$50 K	$94 K+
Securities Analyst	$40-45 K	$100 K+
Insurance Sales	$35 K	$100 K+
Commercial Real Estate Sales	$34 K	$200 K+
Legal Assistant	$21 K	$30 K+

Media Escort/Publicity Liaison	$125 per day	
Fitness Technician	$4-7 per hour	$75 per hour

This chart indicates some of the newer job classifications that have opened up to women, but it also denotes the pay differential. In fairness, it should be considered that the top people in each field may have considerable experience and/or time in service to be worthy of their higher pay.

In other words, since the sixties' revolution, women have made some worthy improvements and upward movement, but they are still restricted to entering traditional fields, except in an extremely selected and limited way, because it is still generally believed that women lack the skills or the intelligence (or both) to learn and maintain a career and a family simultaneously. The media implication here suggests that women can't chew gum and run at the same time. Nonsense! Women, by increasing numbers, are maintaining family, career and even marriage, very successfully and admirably. Men just refuse to admit women's capabilities.

In her article "'Right Stuff' Can Bump against the Glass Ceiling," in *The Chicago Tribune,* Jan. 6, 1992, Carol Klieman reports, "Spalter-Roth, an assistant professor of sociology at American University, says women get lower rewards for their work experience. Top management has a vision of the appropriate person to promote, and every study tells us it's someone who looks like them: middle-age, white, male, and often with a stay-at-home wife. Women and minorities are not seen in the gut or subconscious as the appropriate candidate."

Domination by men will continue until women gain enough clout to override these prejudicial attitudes. Men write the rules and often change them at will to stonewall any challenge to change. They still, in spite of what is said, continue to maintain that privilege. They are most reluctant to lose their advantages or to share them. To avoid intrusion, they fortify their positions and construct rules for distributing awards. This helps keep their dominance intact and helps to keep women segregated. They do indeed control women's pay. Sadly, even as women gain a greater foothold into the male-dominated jobs, they come aboard as *cheaper* labor.

Not only will men try to preserve their authoritative position, but they will resist any effort to improve occupational status or include women in privileged positions. They are too comfortable in their towers and prefer the status quo. "Equal pay for equal work is fraud for women," says Heidi Hartmann in her book, *Capitalism, Patriarchy, and Job Segregation by Sex*. Men still have the power to control the game and keep women off the playing field. They easily can manipulate job interviews, job evaluations and pay scale criteria (comparable worth). When men include a token number of women into the higher ranks and create a false breakthrough, they soon develop an even higher plateau for themselves to prevent the possibility of relinquishing power or control.

How do women overcome this dominance and men's ability to control their career, wages and right to equality?

One woman did it in the following way. I referred earlier to a woman who led the entire U.S. in sales for her company and received awards for it, only to find that her boss had moved a male friend into the sales territory that she had worked long and hard to develop. This was clearly an attempt to destroy her further potential and, obviously, her self-confidence. This woman, unhappy, realized that her performance and achievements were being unrecognized simply because she was a woman, and she chose to relocate to another area for a new beginning, a new challenge, and with a new boss within the same company. The woman, having learned somewhat of a lesson, nimbly developed a solid rapport with a few people in the higher levels of the hierarchy so as to protect her career. I go into more detail concerning this application in Chapter 7. Her old boss was soon forced to realize his error in judgment and he had his responsibility reduced in the form of a demotion. He soon left the company. She resigned a short time later and accepted a position of greater rank, rewards and prestige.

Women can overcome all inequalities if they are patient and persevering. It won't be easy and it strains the emotions but it can be done. All it takes is firm desire and commitment. Yes, the woman in my story took a risk, but one has to do something. You can't just let them get away with their foul play. The difference today is that you have more support than you used to have, either from within the company or by virtue of the possible threat of government intervention.

There *is* a wage gap. It is there for phony reasons, which were concocted to keep you suppressed. Even though there have been small improvements, you must keep the pressure on and never let irresponsible men get away with their illegal acts. Make promises to yourself to be strong and courageous enough to challenge and fight when you know you are being treated poorly and illegally. You have more to gain than to lose.

SYNOPSIS

As you dwell on these thoughts, keep in mind that there is upward growth in status for women and that there is a pronounced trend toward stabilizing and undoing wage atrocities. Those who won't adjust to this change will suffer the loss of very bright, aggressive, young, twenty-first century women, like the one portrayed in this chapter, who, because of her self-commitment, refuses to wait for her twentieth-century boss to conjure up another unfair reason to defer or refuse fair pay. Yet, give her equality and she will produce results, because she knows she is as good as any man and better than most. Follow her lead. Don't be intimidated by reversals. Just learn from your mistakes and maintain a positive posture.

Don't accept a smaller pay check than your male counterpart, either. Don't you for one minute ever think his work is worth more than yours or that he is more capable than you. He is not!

I always wanted to be somebody. If I made it, it's half because I was game enough to take the punishment along the way and half because there were a lot of people who cared enough to help me.
—Althea Gibson

One can never consent to creep when one feels an impulse to soar.
—Helen Keller

4

A Strong Woman Can Overpower a Strong Man

In earlier days, that is, in the seventies and eighties, authors wrote convincingly of the power of self-confidence, of the need for women to adjust to a man's world, of how to think like a man, and so on. They included in their writings some words on proper dress, proper behavior in the office or at the drinking fountain, proper body language and a host of other well-intentioned suggestions. But these didn't work. For every suggestion offered, men countered by developing internal or external barriers. These suggestions proved to be too motherly, overly feminine, intimidating, incompatible with men's surroundings and too easy to challenge—and they were challenged. These offerings served only as band-aids, not the rambunctious attack on the male empire that feminists sought. It still will take a lot more than this. It will require strong individual effort, woman helping woman through a good networking program, and a powerful positive attitude.

Women will have to change men! Men will have to accept the change and learn to live with women in a partnership state as equals in joint interest. Men will have to accept women as peers, as competitors, and as their managers or bosses. The onus is not on women—it's on men. Men may have to swallow a lot of pride and ego before they accept this drastic change in their approach to women. However, they may deny the inevitable and suffer the consequences of not promoting bright, intelligent women, such as those previously mentioned in this book. Whichever way men choose, don't back down or begin to feel sorry for them (another female weakness). In a competitive environment, sensitivity comes in last. Men expect you to cave in. They don't think you have the courage and patience to hang in there. Don't prove them right.

It boils down to this: women must *believe* that they are equal to men. They must adjust their thinking and instincts in order to better position themselves. With all of the hullabaloo in the press, on television and in magazines pointing to equality, there are still many women who continue to accept or even hide behind inferiority and low self-esteem. Pity them—they are condemned to the past.

If you truly want to succeed in any career or worthwhile life adventure dominated by the "good ol' boys," you will not succeed by displaying even the slightest indication of self-doubt. Successful men won't accept it. They don't think like that, because they know it is self-defeating. Women can't afford to think like that either. It is not a male attribute—it is a human requirement. You can't live your life in fear of day-to-day setbacks or surprises. You can't win if you fear the head-to-head challenges that will confront you. You won't succeed at all unless you rid yourself of the negative, stereotypical beliefs with which you were born and raised. You must view this as a rebirth for you and an adventure unto itself.

Don't step aside for any man in your quest for success. You have every right to the good life that he has. Don't fail to challenge him when it is necessary to take a strong position, especially when the position is unpopular. Don't accept second best because you feel that is where you belong. You must learn to walk ahead of him, or at the very least, side by side.

You are aware that some men are proficient at smooth-talking women. *All* men become masters at it when they want to keep you from challenging their domain or winning their spot. Be on guard! Being a victim of this is not uncommon for women. Always consider it as a possible part of his game plan and always keep in mind that in his competitive mind set is the commitment, "I will do whatever it takes to win," just waiting to be enacted.

You, likewise, must adopt this philosophy if you intend to win. Don't spot him any points and expect to catch up later—he won't let you.

Remember that men feel strongly about being Number One. They are constantly reminded and personally challenged into believing that Number One is not only the right place but the only place. Win the big one and you will be remembered; come in second and you will be forgotten. This is their code. Make it your code too.

Now, lift your head up from this book, go to your favorite mirror, and tell yourself:

I AM NUMBER ONE. I AM AS GOOD AS ANY MAN
AND BETTER THAN MOST.
I BELIEVE IN MYSELF AS A WINNER.
I WILL CONTROL MY OWN DESTINY.

Repeat this every day. This is your number one lesson in winning. Anything less will deprive you of all of those extras in life that you have every right to enjoy. *YOU MUST BELIEVE IN YOURSELF.*

If I didn't believe that you or any woman could achieve the highest and the most responsible positions that men achieve, I wouldn't be writing this book. With all of my years of experience working with women, I know the working woman. I know your potential. There isn't a responsible, high-level position in any field that cannot be successfully managed by a woman, and I can think of a number of high-level positions right now that need to be improved upon.

I firmly believe all of this. But the question is, do you?

If you see yourself as a strong, successful human being, then you are well on your way to achieving that success. You must see yourself in that role and be convinced that you want it and can get it. If you see yourself as Number One, are totally committed to being Number One, and are willing to work extremely hard to be Number One, you will achieve Number One.

I firmly believe that, also.

Always Work from Strength!

Because you are a woman, chances are that you possess many important qualities often missing in the workplace. Among them are patience, compassion, a fair and loving approach, and the know-how and know-when to use these special gifts. You are truly blessed, because today these are the qualities that could be the real answers to all of the troubles and problems throughout the world.

You are masters at feeling and sharing love. And it is this virtue that is the common denominator, the real link to overcoming man's inhumanity to others. By your example of all of these special gifts, men will eventually acknowledge your successes and accept your solutions. On the other hand, if you don't see yourself in this illustrious, esteemed position or you fear you just can't make it—you won't. Don't you see how important you are in reshaping the workplace?

Always work from strength, never from weakness! Never say you can't do something. Always say, "Yes, I will, I can." As you gain strength in the eyes of those who supervise or control your career, they will ask many things of you that will seem impossible to achieve. Remember, they wouldn't ask you if they didn't think you could do it, and they only ask you because you have proven to them that you are capable. It's called "paying your dues," and you must do this at every step along the way.

In my thousands of daily decisions during a hectic career of constant change, adjustments, growth, in-fighting, politics and observance of "good ol' boy" abrasive confrontations—tough-mindedness accompanied by a firm resolve were the keys to maintaining proper balance and successfully outlasting the competition or opponent. You can't be a wimp. There is no substitute for mental strength.

Always work from strength!

In practicing this toughness and displaying strength (the products of self-confidence and a good self-image), it is necessary to surround yourself with good people who display similar traits. Join yourself with "yes" people, and everyone quickly recognizes this as a weakness, along with your inability to draw out the best from your associates.

The positive traits of fair play, love, compassion, endearment and attentive listening will bring people closer to you, help you gain their support and confidence and reinforce their vision of you as their strong leader and safeguard of security. It doesn't take a psychic or a prophet to predict strong leadership based on those positive traits mentioned above.

When associates see strength and comfort in your self-assurance and security, they, too, gain further confidence and ultimately an increase in self-confidence. They will know that when things get tough in the workplace, as they often do, many times without warning, they can rely on being led properly with clear expectations. They will know, too, that no matter how tough it gets or what your decisions may be, those will be carefully and professionally made and in their best interest.

***The Golden Parachute Theory of Leadership*:**

- *If you communicate with your people often, they will listen and follow you.*

  Communication—it begins with a "good morning" every day, either one-on-one or in a daily morning meeting. Periodically throughout a work period you must stop at your associates' work areas for a brief chat about work, family or whatever. Give them the chance to talk about themselves, their problems, any suggestions they have or any improvements they would like to recommend.

  It ends with you standing at the exit door each night bidding good night as they return to their families. And, oh yes, please listen intently to what they are saying to you and take notes on things that need your attention.

- *If you work with them, at their side, often—they will respect you as a friend and leader.*

  You need friends in your workplace and you need the respect that goes with it. If you work with them periodically at their job stations, even performing their tasks, your people love it. They now sense you are not above doing their jobs and hence not above them except in title. As you do this with each one, the team takes on a positive attitude toward your goals and toward you as their leader. When the job gets tough or demands increase they will be there with you to see you through to success and will feel good about it.

- *If you provide the necessary tools for them to do their jobs, they will perform beyond your expectations.*

One of the benefits of communicating and actually working with your people is that you learn why they cannot do a specific assignment. They may not have the right tool or the right instructions. They may have misunderstood instructions, or have taken conflicting directions from two or more bosses, or perhaps their questions have never been answered. Provide them with the things they need to perform and their productivity will reach record heights.

- *If you reward their good performances, especially in front of their peers, they will achieve your goals for you.*

  Make a habit of seeking out good work instead of mistakes on things overlooked. Promoting good work promotes good workers. A pat on the back to one of your people is felt by all of your people. You get the reputation of one who cares about them and what they do; whatever you ask them to do will get done and things you never expected to get done will no longer exist.

- *If you seek their help in tough times, they will oblige you with expert advice.*

  You can't do everything yourself, and you will achieve very little without the help of your people. Your people are the experts at their jobs and they should be so informed. Respect that talent by asking for their help, their input in tough matters and during tough times. "I have a real serious problem, and I need your help," is music to their ears, and they will go all out to respond with their expertise. All you have to do is ask them.

- *If you love them, they will know it and will return your love, and they will never fail you.*

  How you are interpreted in the eyes and hearts of your people is determined by what is in *your* eyes and heart. Look on your people with respect, understanding, compassion and a measure of discipline, and they will be quick to know that you care about them. Talk to them honestly and with sincerity on sensitive subjects and those that are close to their hearts. When you really, really care, your people will know. And so will you, because that silent spirit of love will quickly flow back to you. There is nothing in any work more recognized and accepted as the warmth and trust that comes from love.

- *If you must discipline them, do it swiftly, honestly, and fairly.*
  Disciplining your people can also be a sign of love, because correcting them shows them that you really care about them. When your people are neglectful, complacent, not performing to potential or to your expectations, or if they break rules or have an attitude problem, you *must* discipline them. A break down in total discipline will occur in your workplace if you fail in acting swiftly and firmly. When you discipline, have your facts straight and be prepared to substantiate them. Do it one-on-one, in private, in a sound-proof area. Be brief in your accusations and repeat them only once. Make sure your evaluation is honest and thorough and that it would be in keeping with what you would expect from your own boss. Above all you must be fair. Make sure you have studied and weighed both sides. Once completed, forget that it happened and never bring it up again unless the behavior is repeated. One way to close a disciplinary reprimand is by saying, "Now I feel good because I know I will never have to discuss this with you again—isn't that right?"

If you don't like or revere people, particularly your associates, you will never gain the "good manager" status. You can't direct or coach people you don't really like and respect.

If men are a problem, especially with all of the recent men-bashing, and your respect and approval of them is a hang-up, you must adjust. You will never succeed without them. You will never succeed without their support and help.

You must find the good in them and be positive in dealing with them. Don't overlook the fact that men are human and have problems too. Dwell on that as you focus on working together. Success is directly related to your love of self and love of people.

When applying for a job and particularly during interviews (at every level), the most positive statement from almost every applicant is, "I like people; I like working with people." This is a necessary attitude if you are to achieve success. When properly applied, it must come from the heart. Insincerity will be detected quickly, and you will be labeled as a phony.

It is this positive impression that will motivate subordinates and associates either to work extra hard for you or to drag their feet, causing you problems. Liking people is another important ingredient in achieving a successful career.

Your associates are the vital link to your entire accomplishment. You can't get there alone. People will either perform for you because they simply want to, or they will give you their all, their fullest measure, and never say "no" to you because they love you. It's as simple as that. Either way will get you there, but the latter will get you there faster, with more appreciation of them and yourself, including a very special inward happiness. Your boss may also observe and feel good about your actions. He may even be envious because he, like many, may lack the understanding of this basic principle of good leadership. On the other hand, if you ride your people, harass them, treat them disrespectfully or even over-supervise them, your days are numbered.

A common mistake made by people who supervise is their lack of understanding of the importance of visibility with those whom they supervise. Work with them, chat with them, create the work ethic and the tone, set the pace and answer all of their many questions. Make the workplace "family friendly." Let them know you care. This will pay off enormously in respect for you.

All too often I hear managers and supervisors side-step a question or defer it until later. This is a serious error, especially when you tell them, "I will get back to you later." Later usually never comes. Only in very severe circumstances (a customer question or phone call), should their answers be delayed. By not answering questions promptly, you risk your employees' slowing down or stopping their work and, if done repeatedly, their loss of confidence in you. If you want your people to care, you will have to care. People want to do their best and become very upset with interruptions. Assist their progress; don't get in the way of it. This emphasis on motivation, liking people and working with them is my impassioned plea to you. It is a message that should be engraved on your heart as the basis of your everyday life at work.

In a busy workplace, managers find themselves bombarded with frequent questions and people continually seeking advice and direction. However, nothing is more frustrating to an employee than to be put off and forgotten when seeking help and guidance. You don't appreciate it if your boss acts this way and you shouldn't expect anything less from your people.

In a workplace with multiple supervisors, you can always recognize the strongest supervisor. He or she is the one who answers all calls and questions and is always around when needed. This supervisor will be the one whom all employees admire the most, gather around, look up to and go to for advice. These supervisors are also the ones who promote team programs and goals, who make a total commitment to achievement and who take utmost pride in the success of the operations and its people. This is how to gain strength as a boss—something many do not understand or embrace.

You still can't get there alone—but you can get there.

The Great Impostors

Having been in the business arena for so many years, having had the good fortune to be mentored, trained and directed by some giants, and having been associated with other extraordinarily great women and men was as rewarding and cherished an experience as anyone would ever want. My overall memory of the participants is certainly a positive affirmation. Yet one must agree that nothing is always perfect except the Almighty, and we know that with the many that are good, sometimes there appear some who are not so good.

In every entrepreneurship, at one stage or another you will collide with or at best witness the antics of a phony, a fake, an imposter or whatever name you want to call him on that frightful day he does you wrong. This hypocrite will generally lie, cheat, steal and cover-up anything in order to get ahead or make himself look good. He is the one who pretends to like you, but would soon destroy you and your career if it resulted in his advancement. If you watch him, you will find he is adept at avoiding real work and for the most part hasn't the faintest idea how to perform good work in any manner.

You guessed it. I would not be pleased to be in the employ or even in the same room as one of these—nor should you.

Women are generally good at recognizing these phonies. Call it intuition if you want, but women do have an innate perception of the insincerity of these types. Contrarily, some women become willing victims of this scoundrel as they push for personal gain. As a result, they lose and end up suffering insults, degrading treatment, verbal abuse and, worst of all, injury to their reputation.

Very young women are easier prey due to their inexperience and their young, naive, positive expectations of a hearts-and-flowers world in general. When this young group experiences the shenanigans of this character, they generally do an "about face" and begin to reevaluate their thought processes in search of better decisions. It is also at this time that they learn of the power of experience as a teacher.

You will meet with this type somewhere, either as a boss or as a peer. Your plan of defense must be to:

1. Stay as far away as possible;
2. Be sure your work is exemplary and beyond reproach;
3. Document everything—*everything*—that doesn't look or sound right; and
4. Never, but *never,* become part of his shenanigans.

I have seen women fall victim to this type of person a number of times. These impostors falsely present themselves with a woman to gain her confidence so he can eventually steal her ideas and thoughts, gain sexual favors and then gain full support for his thievery or quackery.

Don't be misled by this fool, and don't play up to him as a gimmick to inflate his ego or to promote yourself. You will lose.

Your inherited instincts are strong and will serve you well if you put them to work and trust them. Remember, your first instinct is often correct. Please don't let your adventurous inclinations draw you into his insidious web and subsequently put you into a world of hurt.

To work with or for this individual and really survive, the following tips will help and guide you to safer ground and make your effort manageable:

1) Become a very strong leader with your people and those associates around you. Use the Golden Parachute of Leadership principle (see Chapter 5) as your reference and guide. Remember you are at least his equal. More than that, you possess a deeper, more worthy character. Be right up front when it comes to your opinion about him and his games. He may become disturbed, but he also knows where you stand.

2) Work toward becoming the authority in your job function and also become a good student of his job function.

This way you are ahead of him and are better able to judge when he may be setting you up or misleading you into a wrong direction.

3) Work from strength (my favorite) and take control in discussions so you can guide him away from disingenuous thoughts and ideas.

You as a woman have the unique ability to control most situations when you really want to. You have special strengths, such as knowing when to say what you think and when to keep mum, when to compliment and when to go silent, when to disappear and when to be oblivious of your surroundings, and then again when to take the limelight. Most men don't know this and when they see this action, it scares them. Use these strengths when dealing with the great imposter.

Work from strength and don't fear retaliation or denial. If it comes, reject it and continue toward becoming Number One. You, as a woman, are unique and have important and needed values and strengths. Find them; put them to work. They will give you the needed edge.

Be good to your people; never let them down, and always be there when they need you—they will reach out to you often.

Never trust a phony but, in the words of Oscar Wilde:

"Always forgive your enemies;
nothing annoys them so much."

SYNOPSIS

Women will have to change men and men will have to accept the change. The process is already taking place, as in the parameters for electing government officials, where women are seriously involved as the wives of presidents and vice-presidents. It could be that soon a wife of a candidate may swing the election.

Yes, a strong woman can overpower a strong man and when women overcome the negative, stereotypical "ball and chain" they are born and raised with, you begin to see the winning attitude, the work-from-strength approach, and the other positive traits of fair play, love, compassion, endearment and attentive listening set into motion. These will provide different leadership—the kind that the Golden Parachute of Leadership professes. Love is the emphasis here. It is time for that. There is no one more capable of instilling and using love than a woman. No one relates to love better than men and it is with this in mind that the strength of a woman—love—can indeed overpower a strong man—with love.

Always associate with the best.
—Henry Ford

No theory of unfitness, no form of conventionality, can have the right to suppress any excellence which nature has seen fit to evolve.
—Antoinelle Brown Blackwell

We must not only give what we have; we must give what we are.
—Desire Joseph Cardinal Merrier

5

Love, Marriage and Career

It is easier for the single woman to greet and accept the challenge of a demanding career. Even within a love relationship, the demands of a career plus family still do not exist. It is only when all of this comes together—love, marriage and a career—that the plot thickens and the situation becomes more complex, and sometimes heart-rending. The decision of a single woman affects only one; the career of a married woman affects many, sometimes even those outside the immediate household. The emphasis in this chapter is on the married woman.

Career success requires some necessary decisions. To have it your way, and to prevent your life from falling into the second-rate existence that women for centuries have suffered, may require you to take the initiative and become aggressive in your planning and communicating when it comes to love and marriage. Although this book is directed to the heterosexual persuasion, the content of this chapter can be adjusted by any couple for their own purposes. The focus is not on sex, but rather on living a life with someone, enjoying the fruits of a good relationship, filling your life with positive, happy rewards and achieving your career and marriage plans to the fullest.

You are entitled to the contemporary reformed status for women. Like anyone else, women now have the luxury of deciding for themselves what they want from life. The dominance of men shouldn't be allowed to preclude your thinking and decision-making. You needn't compromise anything. If you are married, discuss your total thinking with your partner and reach a common ground. For you to intermingle domestic life with a career requires extra sacrifice. How big a sacrifice you make will be in direct proportion to the rewards you receive. The bigger the sacrifice, the bigger the rewards.

Women have to choose early on the depth of their sacrifice toward a career. They can't afford to procrastinate for a few years to decide. Men are not hurried like that and, consequently, they can enjoy a few years dwelling on and thinking about the future. If women wait, they chance the loss of a portion of their future either temporarily or altogether. A number of times I have seen women confuse personal life with career life because they delayed their decisions. This can and has resulted in the changing of both their goals and their positive attitude toward themselves and the future. They begin to vascillate and become vulnerable to suggestions that would direct them back to the life of the suppressed, dependent woman, or to a life that will not enable them to take advantage of their natural talents and abilities. If it's marriage, a career, or a career and marriage, all are options and firm possibilities not previously available to women. Caution—you can be very easily side-tracked if you don't display a firm attitude toward your career independence. Don't let male dominance influence your commitment to yourself.

Prepare Yourself

Education beyond high school is a must if you plan any career other than self-employment. A full degree or more will increase your chances measurably. Remember, you will be competing mostly with men who know that education is the key to any successful career. Strong people learn and practice good communication skills and develop strong vocabularies. At the start, a woman already has more to overcome than a man to be "successful." Lack of a good formal education will destroy your chances of anything truly worthwhile. Also, if you do not pursue your education, you are giving the "good ol' boys" another excuse to hold you back or slow your career. Many men who control careers are quick to pounce on an excuse to slow or even destroy a woman's progress. This unfairness has been the subject of noteworthy reports and in the media since the early nineties. Women absolutely cannot create barriers to their progress. The fewer you have, the less time you lose in trying to catch up and the more time you gain for promoting yourself and your efforts.

A Role Model For a Happy Career/Marriage

One successful woman whom I have had the privilege of knowing through most of her career development can serve as an ideal model and example of the married woman with a family and a husband who likewise enjoys an outstanding career. Her original goal was to be an attorney. She obtained a degree in political science. She later relinquished this goal to pursue marriage and raise a family. She is currently a general manager of a large volume department store in the midwest. She has a little girl. This marriage with a career, including the child, has been very successful. It was planned by both partners and they are committed to achieving happiness and success.

The couple shares domestic responsibilities. They share the raising of the child. The child is very much aware that she is loved and enjoys a normal, healthy attitude because she is included in all plans and the commitment made by both parents.

The answer to a successful career/marriage with children is directly related to the treatment and attention given to the children. In this example, the obvious love for the child dictated the parents' career direction. As they created their plans, they included the child at each step, communicated their innermost desires and came to a common ground intelligently. They are equal in their arrangement and as a result have a happy marriage, a happy, contented child and an ideal home life. The key to their successful career/marriage is their ability to communicate. None of this would have been successfully achieved without the give-and-take of good, sound, honest discussion.

Yes, this woman gave up becoming an attorney, but not because she bowed to a hegemonic husband or because she was a surrendering woman. She opted to change course and get married because they talked it out and selected that path. This woman is not sacrificing above and beyond while her husband does his own thing.

I suggest you emulate this couple and subscribe to their wisdom, perseverance and dedication to each other and their family-friendly purpose. They are a great example to follow. Of course, your results might be different. It's the process that is important and the communication that keeps it on target. Because of this couple's careful communication, planning and follow-through, this woman now enjoys a wealth of self-confidence and excels as a role model of self-esteem. She is indeed an ideal model for the married career woman and her husband serves as a model for men as well. There is no question that others have successfully achieved this type of arrangement. Married couples should find comfort in knowing that many have overcome the obstacles to a more equitable relationship and that the possibility for combined success is just a conversation away.

You must expect and prepare for problems and controversy as you face the future as a career seeker. You must enter this phase with an open mind, considering all of your options, and plan and chart the course you want to take. Look for happiness as well as success or material fulfillment. You do have options. Don't let anything prevent you from choosing or using them. Many women are succeeding today even though they had encountered seemingly insurmountable problems getting their man or partner to adjust. Men will change if they want you to succeed badly enough. They are more flexible than they appear. They will love you more as they see your wise decisions blossom into a successful, happy, rewarding career. They may even be proud of themselves for choosing such an aggressive, successful woman. True love is on your side and will work hard for both of you.

Choosing a Spouse

Consider carefully who you choose to have a partnership with because you will not achieve total career success if you insist upon marrying a man who demands a strict, traditional "dinner on the table at six" washer/dryer attendant, or who exhibits a "Bring me a beer!" attitude, while you go at break-neck speed trying to master all of the demands of his will and those of the rest of the family. This is what most men expect because (1) society is still sending conflicting messages to both men and women and (2) most men still live in the traditional life. It isn't their fault. That's what they saw and learned. It isn't, however, the way it should be or will be if you make your position known, stand your ground firmly on the most desired issues and make your mate feel wanted.

You can achieve much more if you choose a partnership/marriage with a man who already understands and is willing to accept the new entrepreneurial woman, including new thoughts and ideas on marriage. A successful marriage is a tough assignment for everyone. It has many known and unknown problems. It comes with surprises, frustrations, disasters, emergencies and challenges. It isn't easy—but it is fun. It is a 50-50 sharing, not a 90-10 burden. However, the failure to work all this out prior to walking to the altar can put you in a very long, unhappy and unfulfilled life.

If you have married and did not include this career dialogue in the prenuptial discussions or engagement, you will need to begin to create a foundation for this discussion in a positive way. Chances are it will be difficult for him to understand how important a career is to you and that you, like him, are entitled to it and to becoming a whole person. A positive dialogue with an established, firm commitment must be your major goal with guarantees to prevent his regression back to traditionalism. To win this one will require your best effort.

Again, marriage is a 50-50 obligation. This is not just a numeric equation. There is no way you can career-it as a 60-40 or 70-30 housewife. The demands are far too challenging. You will need to divide domestic responsibilities as our woman general manager did, and you will need cooperation and a well-thought-out plan.

Programming him should be basic and should not be so strict that he envisions all of his male activities being sacrificed. Sacrifices he will make, but golf is still golf. He still has an ego and is *still entitled to his fair share* and his point of view. To leave room for compromise is wise indeed, and the woman who knows this has the mark of a successful executive.

The Reward

The rewards of a two-career family are numerous. The luxury of two incomes and the fulfillment of helping each other achieve your dreams while still maintaining a family life will be an enviable accomplishment, something to shout about.

Keep in mind that give-and-take is continually required. Career goals are easier to give up than to achieve. Sometimes it's easier to yield to tradition than to stand up for your rights. If you are committed to wanting a career, you can have it. All of this will not be easy—nothing worthwhile ever is. Elevating women to equal status or to a position that will forever change men's minds is a task unparalleled in history. It will take hard work, commitment and understanding by all. The key to the success of all of this is found in the strength of your commitment. Either you have a total dedication to your career goal or you don't. There are no maybes to this cause. Any sign of weakness could lead you away from your goal.

If you came to this chapter expecting a quick-fix to your career/marriage problems, you now know there aren't any listed. The circumstances surrounding each individual career/marriage can be as diverse as the number of couples involved. Consequently, I cannot guide you to a quick-fix list of answers to these problems. In each case, however, the solution can be reached by the same method, communication—real, honest communication, the give-and-take type, where you listen more than you talk and approach the conversation with an open mind and heart, geared toward total solution, sincerity and complete honesty. On the other hand, I wouldn't propose any of this if I hadn't already witnessed its success in action. While couples are working on solutions to their problems, involved companies, and even our governments, are increasing their efforts to help women enter and remain in the work force.

As men read this chapter, some will probably be outraged at the suggestions and directions. Be prepared and consider their rebuttal as you reinforce your own plans and thinking from a woman's point of view.

Remember, it is important that you have a plan and that you articulate that idea to the person in your partnership. Before you begin the partnership *this needs to be well thought-out.*

Frequently, as I hear men discuss their marriages, wives, shared duties and the rest, there is an obvious attitude change toward the partnership as a team effort—the way things ought to be. Men *are* changing.

I recently listened to a man refuse a relocation assignment from his employer that in turn would lead to the next promotion. He did this because his wife's position was blossoming rapidly and he didn't want her to suffer the loss of a rewarding career. This couple has an agreement that when one of the careers becomes more important than the other, they protect the advancing one. One has to admit this is a change from traditional roles. It appears that this woman is being afforded equal treatment—which all women have been trying to achieve for centuries.

I could go on with many examples where men have used good judgment and favored their spouses' budding careers. These are different times with a new age and a new approach to love, marriage and a career. Do men lose? Absolutely not. If the process is correctly programmed with well-thought-out parameters, there need not be any losers—as long as those involved continue to communicate their thoughts and ideas.

There are many good men out there who are unselfish and who recognize how intelligent and capable women can be. Because of their own self-worth and self-confidence, these men should not fear the competition, but rather find it interesting and a tremendous human adventure.

SYNOPSIS

For the married woman, a strong approach toward priorities is mandatory. A strong sense of emotional balance is a must, and a firm commitment together with a well-thought-out plan is paramount. While none of these will ensure success, miss any one of them and you will reap a heavy burden and eventually risk failure. The road to success by any woman is not easy. Nothing worthwhile ever is.

On the other hand, some women, because they had good judgment, exercised patience and used common sense when choosing a mate, find so much support that their careers are made simpler and climbing the career ladder becomes not only a monetary reward but a wondrous adventure.

A career-plus-marriage can take any route you desire. The key is honest communication of your sincerest thoughts to each other, then patient overcoming of the obstacles this produces. It worked for the department store general manager. It can work for you, too.

The new age for men and women as married couples is slowly taking a turn toward accommodation, coequality and compatibility, as well as sufficient independence and space for each partner to feel individual. Could we be approaching a new age of reasoning and common sense coupled with love?

However, we still hear from those who claim the old way is best: a woman belongs in the home, raising the kids, serving her man. This approach is being preached throughout the media and will crop up occasionally. Be advised that this is considered to be the unrelenting work of male dominance that fears and refuses to accept a woman as an equal. Nonetheless, most women are overjoyed that they are finally being recognized.

If it is your choice to stay at home, raise the kids, and so on, that's O.K. But don't be misled by the media that this is the most popular choice of women, or make your choice based on that misleading propaganda.

Think first, ye women, to look to your behavior.
The face pleases when character commends.
Love of character is lasting;
beauty will be ravaged by age.
—Ovid

6

Beauty Can Be the Beast

As a man, I know that most men fear women when they are competing in the workplace. It is the underlying reason that the "glass ceiling" exists in the first place. It is the reason that men cannot get comfortable when a woman becomes part of their team. It is the reason men resort to put-downs, disrespectful comments, and ultimately to chauvinistic shenanigans in order to live with them on the job. Fact is, men don't know how to deal with women. If you are a beautiful woman physically, you have the edge. If you are not, you probably wish that you were. Don't grieve over this, most aren't. Those who are owe a great deal of thanks to their ancestors and the many enhancers advertised in the marketplace. However, sometimes beauty can be a disadvantage.

Men love beauty. Some won't admit this. Often influential men will praise their employees by calling them "beautiful people." It is considered a nice phrase, intended to "up the spirits" of the group, capture some togetherness and build group esteem. Still other men of influence can be uncomplimentary in reference to the beauty of women. Take John Ruskin, for example, who said:

"The most beautiful things in the world
are the most useless;
peacocks and lilies, for instance."

Real beauty of character, the kind that gains the love and respect of associates, peers and others in the workplace, is an asset. It allows you to take advantage of your positive mental and spiritual values and use them to your overall advantage.

Time will run out on physical beauty; it rarely lasts forever. If it does, it costs a fortune. Furthermore, it takes valuable hours from women that they spend on adjusting what they see in the mirror. Still more time is spent on their hair or at the hairdresser's and in shopping for "just the right look" in clothes. Then a good deal of time and energy are exerted in going out of their way just to get complimented.

At any rate, those beautiful in mind and spirit can save all of that time and put it to good use by applying it to their careers and stretching the distance between themselves and their peers in career competition.

The most successful women are those who are unafraid to get into the job, "get dirty," so to speak, and get stained with grass roots experience and knowledge. This is the stuff that those seeking higher positions are sometimes too weak-kneed to do. They flunk learning and practicing the real measure of a good boss or supervisor. Unfortunately, there are some women in supervisory positions who fall into this category and consequently find the going rough as a result. If you want to excel in leadership, be a real asset to your company and your working relationships, and prepare yourself for the opportunity of very high office, then you must divorce yourself from this "junk-thinking" shortcut method of instant success. It doesn't work, *only hard work works.*

Many times a beautiful woman in charge tries to take a short cut to success by misusing subordinates (*i.e.,* requiring that subordinates perform her supervisory tasks, work longer hours than reasonable, be more committed than subordinate salary will allow, and so on and so forth). By misusing her position either she feels secure that her beauty is all that interests her male boss, or she intimidates those around her into thinking she reigns supreme because of her beauty.

This attitude can lead a beautiful woman to (1) purposely avoid performing important, responsible, every day tasks (she calls them boring); (2) create a false sense of job security whereby she now avoids getting dirty, getting down into the job; and (3) display an attitude that she is above her work and far above those who report to her.

Physically performing every job you ask of a subordinate or trainee is the only acceptable criteria that allows you to direct him/her to do these tasks. How can you expect subordinates to do a job that you won't or can't do yourself? How can you expect them to perform properly and to your satisfaction if you are incapable of training them because you do not know the correct way to do it? Your beauty will not give you an iota of help when the demand is for hands-on knowledge and experience. You don't know what the job is until *you* have done it. Try and fake your way through and you lose. Your people will find you out and your boss will destroy you. You cannot afford to avoid this step. So don't pretend to be another Cleopatra and rely on beauty to lead. Rely on hard-earned, job know-how. You certainly will not survive in tomorrow's world if you attempt to leave an impression that you are above doing the work, and you certainly won't survive if you rely on beauty alone for success.

Each job you perform prepares you for the next. A good C.E.O. is one who knows by sight how long it takes to perform the job of each associate in his command, at any level. Beauty means nothing to him, the only thing that counts is results.

Program yourself with that in mind as you pass up the majority of supposedly competent men who challenge you for promotion. Men are geared toward instant success. It's something they have learned to expect as they watched key sports figures demand and receive millions for sometimes inferior performances. As a result, there are no Joe DiMaggios in baseball today, mostly just overpaid minor-leaguers.

There are no shortcuts to visible, high-level positions. It takes hard work. Getting promoted and eventually breaking that "glass ceiling" isn't done with "pretty" (unless you marry the owner); it is done only with long hours and total commitment. Don't expect it any other way. That is why I suggested earlier that you will need to work especially hard in order to succeed. So many setbacks can derail you if you let them. This applies regardless of gender. If men can do it, so can you.

If you were blessed with good looks and misuse these attributes as a means of improving your job position, you are a fool. Learned knowledge and skill in applying it is the edge you need in tough competition. Use all your time furthering this rather than wasting time primping for the boss. Skill is the only real advantage you have when times get tough and cutbacks or layoffs arrive. A company or institution pays you for what you know and for achieved results, not for having a pretty face.

In today's working atmosphere, most women want acknowledgment for the hard, honest work they perform, not for how great they look. A compliment about the beauty of one's eyes is one thing. Recognizing an outstanding job is better, and I hope this will soon become the standard of the future.

I believe that what women resent
is not so much giving herself in pieces
as giving herself purposelessly.
—Anne Morrow Lindberg

SYNOPSIS

Does beauty really become an asset when you are seeking a real career? Does it really add anything to your true character? Or does beauty contribute to an extra problem for an aspiring woman?

This chapter spells out for you that beauty can be an asset, especially if you use it advantageously and don't simply adorn yourself with the material benefits it offers. Most men are intimidated by beauty because it distracts them from the interests and issues at hand. This distraction can be useful to you when trying to make your point in an argument or deep discussion. A momentary thought about your beauty may be just enough to disarm their thoughts and weaken them to give in and say "yes" to your ideas. But, remember, this is called "playing games" and, while it works, it isn't a long-term formula for an honest, stable, quality career.

Beauty can be your beast if you use it to promote yourself on its strengths rather than on the character of the beautiful woman you have worked so hard to develop since being a little girl.

Many men will fall for your beauty and will make you feel special and give you false hope of real career progress. This momentary relapse by a man will not last, because at some point he will be drawn back to reality and remember that companies rise or fall on the results of the players. If you replace quality performance with beauty, you become the fool and are now a weak link to the "bottom line." In other words, you are now on the future casualty list.

Job performance, your success in working with people, how well you plan your work, your self-confidence, self-esteem, attitude, team play and personal commitment—these are the ingredients that increase your bottom-line and make you the winner, the key player, the right one for that great new assignment. Do you want career advancement, promotions, great job assignments? Then promote that great person you are and save the beauty until after six.

There are no shortcuts to supreme success. It takes hard work, commitment to excellence and a dedicated attitude. You do, indeed, have all of the ingredients. All you have to do is develop the right ones.

I suggest that you be among those beautiful women who choose to have men and bosses offer compliments and accolades for your good, intelligent performance, and that you forgo reliance on your beautiful physical attributes. Accept compliments for what they really are, then show your male boss the results of your great work, goals achieved, and new ideas that will help him become more successful and the company more profitable. That is the name of the game. Nothing else need be addressed.

The first commandment is:
don't let them scare you.
—Elmer Davis

Manliness is not all swagger and swearing and
mountain climbing. Manliness is also
tenderness, gentleness, consideration.
You men think you can decide on who is a man,
when only a woman can really know.
—Robert Anderson

7

How the "Good Ol' Boy" System Works

Neither men nor women come into this world with the knowledge, experience or other necessities that insure success. It's what happens after "day one" that develops physical and mental strengths, attitudes and aptitudes that mold men or women into successful entrepreneurs or leaders.

Men, from the beginning, are awarded a special bonus simply because they are men. This has irked all women at one time or another. This special treatment has raised man's self-esteem to where he visualizes himself as superior. Women are the victims of a man's traditional upbringing and male child training.

The traditional male upbringing includes inculcation with the work ethic and exposure to role models. Role models have a special influence on men, who have enjoyed this advantage since early childhood. Many successful men have fathers who served as positive role models and boys and young men have always had strong mentors in sports, in business, in their spiritual life and in most other character-building pursuits.

Again, women are at a disadvantage when it comes to role model/mentor selection. While some top role models have surfaced in the past decade or so, their impact has never survived to the point where women try to emulate them to any great degree. Other than a few Olympic greats and other outstanding athletes, women have been given very few strong role models. You are and always have been expected to be feminine and just a woman. You have been forcibly satisfied with this. You are seldom permitted to excel in important quality decisions or to take charge, wield power, propose change or break any workplace records. It has been difficult to develop role models, given these restrictions. Again, you need the advantages that come from networking and committing to help each other. Men do that. Women will have to also, but too seldom do now. In fact, they often work against other women—considering them a threat. Hey, this is no time to be a loner. You need each other now more than ever before. Furthermore, you will have to visualize yourself as a pioneer for other women and prepare yourself to accept with calm equanimity the criticism and jealousy that will come with it, without letting such negative distractions derail or disturb your forward momentum.

You will be required to be a stronger person, better prepared than ever before to wage the hard battle in a fight that actually began in the 1890s and lay dormant for decades. Now with a strong affirmative action policy, civil rights laws, and the latest 1991 amendment, you are better positioned to effect change for equalization and to share the good life and good jobs which only men have enjoyed before.

Don't look for an army of women to suddenly appear with banners to help you. It won't happen in the workplace, at least not for a long time. Men still have the control and power. You will have to win it from them one position at a time until enough women are in enough important places to be able to effect widespread changes more rapidly. The few improvements you see now are there because men have been forced to retreat. You must keep the pressure on.

All you want is an equal chance to perform jobs as men would. Men know this. They also fearfully know that you are capable, and they will not lay down and die or just go away. Most men are still basically chauvinistic and do not want to change. You will need to fight harder because they know what they can lose. They know the good life and how to enjoy the elite positions. You will need the "learn-to-know-what-good-is" theory (see chapter 8) and capture the advantages it offers.

A head-to-head confrontation must be waged daily in the workplace. You must carry it to the highest levels of management, so that everyone, including other women, will know you are something to be reckoned with and are capable and strong with the intent to win. You must never let them destroy your purpose or commitment. You must be a strong role model for other women around you. This is the way women have to be to insure that changes are made and the system overhauled in your favor.

Women know what love is. H.L. Mencken says,

Love is like war. Easy to begin but very hard to stop.

But, Voltaire said,

God is always on the side of the strongest battalion.

With this in mind, I offer encouragement, direction and the following workable tools to move you to win. As long as men continue to dominate you, in some instances ruthlessly and unfairly, this conflict is inevitable, but the challenge must be met.

Lesson I: It Begins With a Change in Attitude

The offensive has begun and a few women have won a few battles. Some minds have been changed. Men look at things a little differently as a result. These few women, instead of being relegated to lowly positions with minimum pay, now enjoy a higher status, more influence and more power.

The women who challenged the "good ol' boys" and won, did so because they no longer accepted "junk thinking," the kind of thinking that permits men to keep women suppressed and convinced that such is their place and purpose in life. This male, domineering approach surfaces occasionally with an attempt to return women to the past. Be alert to this action, challenge it and don't give in.

These pioneering women established themselves as having more worth, and they developed the savvy to deliver that message. They set high standards and goals and persevered, persevered, persevered until they received the attention and recognition due them.

When you chart your own course, plan to get away from the negative thinkers, the naysayers, the weak, the skeptical and those uncommitted to high performance in the workplace. Force yourself to close your ears to gossipers and to those who congregate for negative conversation. Their sole aim, conscious or not, is to keep the downtrodden down and to destroy the self-esteem and self-confidence of the individual, including their own. I urge you to stay away from women (and men) who, because of their lazy habits and thinking, refuse to climb out of their ruts and who want as much company in them as they can get. This is a negative form of power-wielding, the only form known to these people, and engaging in or even listening to it will lead you nowhere but to the minimum wage, the lowest rung on the ladder, or low self-esteem.

Be Loyal and Support Your Employer

As Elbert Hubbard said,

> Remember this. If you work for a man, in heaven's name, work for him. If he pays you wages which supply you bread and butter, work for him; speak well of him; stand by him and stand by the institution he represents. If put in a pinch, an ounce of loyalty is worth a pound of cleverness. If you must vilify, condemn and eternally disparage—resign your position, and when you are on the outside, damn to your heart's content, but as long as you are part of the institution, do not condemn it.

The attitudes of dutiful work and loyalty to your organization are essential to you in your career progress. Successful women learned this lesson early on and found themselves among progressive, free thinkers. This positioned them mentally to proceed on to successful careers. They learned to accept messages, directives and philosophies from direct contact (written or verbal) with higher authority or decision-makers only, and they refused to credit rumors or negative talk. This kept them from getting important information second-hand where intentional or non-intentional changes in the original contents usually occur. The "Did-you-hear-the-latest?" gossip was politely rejected as they excused themselves from such conversations. They had to put themselves above this group or chance jeopardizing their ultimate purpose.

Further, these women commandeered the help of enough progressive, powerful men whose foresight, intelligence and common sense fostered the recognition of women not as the enemy but as equals, not as the weak, dull-witted, manipulating conquerors some men proclaim, but as tremendous assets and total participants in the overall success of all projects.

These women educated themselves to know and identify higher standards because they worked closely enough with their subordinates to recognize their day-to-day problems and to know which ones needed immediate correction and attention. They put themselves in a hands-on working position and, as a result, were better able to recognize low standards in a particular workplace.

Until you learn and submit yourself to the "know-what-good-is" theory (see chapter 8), you will never know or be able to recognize why your idea of hard work is ineffective and unacceptable in the eyes of your boss. You will never know or understand what is really expected of you, what the goals really are, or how to be on a competitive plateau with your adversaries. You can't play the game with the expectation of winning if you can't identify the plan, the players or the goal.

Lesson II: Men Simply Change the Rules

In the past, and in some workplaces even today, the goals and the plans were, and still are, purposely kept from you because you are a woman. Men just don't want women around. They were and still are afraid of women. Men don't want to have their dynasties invaded or to be forced to clean up their acts. They hold their cards close to the vest to protect their male dominance.

Although women and men are better integrated in the workplace today, they are still separated in principle and in how they view each other. Many men still don't understand that women have rights and have much to offer mentally. They debase women's quality performances, productivity and talents.

You need to learn that you simply cannot win by playing their game. You are not on a level playing field. You must take all of this into consideration early on if you plan to wage an aggressive and serious challenge to be the best. Remember though, it is easier today than it was twenty years ago and should continue to improve. Don't despair—hang in there!

Again, don't be misled by the few acceptances men have made in the early seventies and eighties and even now in the nineties. So far, the only true accomplishment you have achieved is to move slightly forward from the back of the bus. You are still only permitted to be a woman in a man's world. Few men and few organizations have broken that mold. But the bondage can be broken on an individual basis.

Sex Discrimination Still Exists!

Physical separation still exists in most work areas and is still being promoted. Today the old guard group of traditionalists doesn't care how close women get, as long as they don't have the opportunity to actually reach the men's level. The younger, more savvy, better-educated men will more readily accept you and maybe even step aside so you can achieve new heights. However, some still have a problem working next to you. The new perception of women does not coincide with what they were taught and what once was—the continuing male dominance that they learned in early life and which they are expected to protect. Use this inner conflict on their part to your advantage and acknowledge any help or positive reinforcement they offer. Take full advantage of any opening you observe.

Men will tolerate your presence in a predominantly male-oriented workplace if you are performing women's jobs. However, they do vehemently resist when women move into "male" jobs. This protective philosophy illustrates the purpose of the "glass ceiling" theory. It is indeed sex discrimination.

As you move up and hold more managerial positions (and I feel strongly that this book will help many do this), there exists that invisible shield, the glass ceiling, that blocks you from moving up, from reaching the door that says "Senior Vice President" or "Chief Executive Officer." Men have purposely insulated themselves from you by continually changing the rules of entry and the rules of the game in general. It is their way of maintaining control and making sure men are the only ones who continue to enjoy the power. Be cognizant of this and alert to it.

Even when you have been accepted into predominantly male fields of employment such as pharmacy, many areas of medicine, computers, construction, car sales or certain factory work—often times those higher up will change your job's status or make adjustments so that certain functions still remain out of your reach. In many instances, these basic changes are the required criteria for promotion to higher positions, which has the effect of blocking you from promotions—and the cover-up will be, "Women just aren't capable or strong enough."

On the whole, women pharmacists are confined to drug stores, drug discount stores and the retail trade. Male pharmacists reach better paying management jobs and the prestige research assignments. Retailing always was considered women's work except in those positions that are better paid or are in middle-to-upper management. Very few women progress past middle management. Here men use the excuse, "Who will do her work when she gets pregnant?" or, "She won't transfer."

Real estate agencies, once dominated by men, have relinquished some of their prestige positions to women. In this field, you came on strong, with astounding success. Today it is common to see 50% of the real estate agencies in any given region owned or managed by women. Women realtors gained expertise, experience and professionalism. As a result of your perseverance and commitment, your self-confidence, self-esteem, self-love and self-worth all blossomed and continue to manifest themselves in the luxuries we all dream about: beautiful homes, high-priced luxury cars, beautiful clothes and other nice amenities once only affordable by men. In addition and most important, a great feeling of self-worth accompanied this growth.

But wait a minute!

Not everything in real estate is open to women. Men had to stop women at some level. They had to find some safe ground on which you can't compete. For this, they now choose the lucrative, high-profile, commercial real estate arena. This segment of real estate requires heavy negotiation. It admits only the "good ol' boys," the million dollar (plus) executives who will not negotiate with women. Very few women are ever seen in this sanctuary making deals. The "good ol' boys" would be at a complete disadvantage if you were to show up for negotiations.

Men educated in computer science with all of its various spinoffs go into turmoil when you walk into their workplace. This robust industry continues to keep you confined in minor roles and prevents you from becoming too much of a factor. They, likewise, have practiced the art of insulating themselves so that they don't have to compete with you.

I have had the opportunity to work with a few good women in this field. I found them excellent, very skillful and a pleasure to work with. Intricate problems are frequent in the computer industry, but proved not too difficult for these women. They solved them as efficiently as any man. I rate these women as more professional, with more compassion, in solving problems when interfacing with laymen. They certainly have more patience. They tend to use more positive reinforcement with those of lesser knowledge. When computers go off-line, they apply more understanding, especially when time and deadlines are a factor. I hail those computer-professional women who got me through troubled times. I thank them again for their help. It is certainly comforting when your computer goes down to know that a knowledgeable woman is standing by to calm you and give you the needed guidance to eliminate your problem and get you back on line.

Forewarned Is Forearmed

Another version of the rule-changing game comes with those bosses who will purposely misdirect your efforts so as to take you out of the mainstream of recognition. These typically take advantage of your hard work and then change the game plan so that you lose participation with the group. This may sound far-fetched, but you'll have to trust me on this one. Let me cite an example:

I recently worked with a woman who was long overdue for promotion and recognition for her outstanding work. She was and still is considered an authority in her job. Her story remains a classic when it comes to manipulation of women in contemporary America. Not only did she go unrecognized (only because she is a woman) but was purposely forgotten when assignments were given out on major new projects or on any prestigiously recognizable project. She continued to work with high standards but was working on the wrong project; she couldn't identify the real game plan or the main goal. When the "thanks" and "great work" compliments were passed out, she was passed up because she was not on the contributing list.

Can this really happen? You bet it can and frequently.

In another situation, I know a woman who has worked for four major Fortune 1000 companies and has moved from one to the other because she failed to be identified with major projects or assignments. In some situations she was given special tasks, but they were away from the main company project and were assignments that no one else would accept.

In each company she was promised equal recognition along with future assignments commensurate with her experience and expertise. It never happened.

Lesson III: Women Have Natural Resources

You, a woman, are capable of doing anything you want to do. I know you are. I have seen and observed you thousands of times in action. You must believe in yourself, however, and feel secure that you are capable and can play the game as well as anyone. Don't listen to those who mistakenly treat you as an inferior. It has been my privilege and rewarding experience to have worked with many women who met or exceeded the required criteria to prove themselves, and who advanced to heights previously unattainable by women at any other time in history.

At the hourly-pay level, I worked with many women who performed repetitious, physically-demanding jobs requiring lengthy, total concentration, and they performed with an attitude that was astounding. Many men doing the same job would be quick to find a way around the work, waiting for a break to goof off or just drag their feet, uncommitted to the job. This I have often experienced as well, to my dismay.

I have worked with, trained or mentored thousands of women who, by their choice, worked in the hourly ranks. Others sought management positions as well as entry-level management positions. They pleaded for career training and promotion into management and supervisory positions. I can tell you with all honesty that women have a better overall attitude toward learning new things and they are easier to work with and faster to train. Many of these trained dynamos are still parked in lower jobs waiting for their chance to prove abilities of *outstanding successful* entrepreneurship. Most have better credentials and exceed the experience of their male counterparts. Unfortunately, I watched them lose out simply because they were women. When will it stop?

Lesson IV: Men Just Don't Get It

None of the women I have mentioned ever had the privilege of sitting behind a door with the title Regional Manager, Assistant Vice President, President or any other top level positions. We all know that this is not a result of lack of brain power or ability. It is just a matter of gender and the practice of segregating of women away from male-dominated chambers.

I have seen women marooned in jobs for years who were fully capable of going higher. Some even advanced their education in anticipation of job promotions. I have seen the frustration in their faces as they were turned away or, in some cases, not even considered when those promotions became available. Believe me, I felt and shared their frustration right along with them.

You know, men just don't get it.

They just don't know the frustration and hurt they impose on you and the destruction of will and self-confidence that results. They see you only as subjected beings who matter only when it fits their need. I see you as a force to be reckoned with someday soon. I also see you as a tower of strength and intelligence that will improve the status and quality of this country. I see you as a catalyst to social change.

You have to become more aggressive as you move toward acceptance in better jobs and in unclaimed fields. *Aggressiveness and risk-taking* are two "non-female" words that must be studied, practiced and mastered by women and eventually removed as deterrents to progress. This is not going to be easy.

During the in-fighting, men use these two characteristics as anti-women labels. They are mentally schooled to look for and quickly recognize any and all small or large signs of aggressive weakness. Stay away from men who suggest you can't do a specific job because it's too tough and really man's work. Watch out for those who would like to pigeonhole you into desk jobs so that they don't have to deal with you in the field. It's common language for men to be heard predicting about women, "She can't hack it"; "When things get tough, she will head for the powder room"; or "Women belong in the home." You must be on guard against these men, who you can best recognize from your own response to them when you find yourself thinking, "They just don't get it!" Your only strategy to overcome such prejudice is knowing ahead of time what you must do, what is required of you, how to achieve it, and to what the results will lead.

Keep your fears to yourself,
but share your courage with others.
—Robert Louis Stevenson

Lesson V: Networking

Furthermore, you can't let other women ridicule your efforts to improve. Some women are lazy and are happy being treated as second-class citizens. Ignore them and don't let them slow your confidence and perseverance. Yes, they will capitalize on the overall gains you make for women. They will cash in after all the work is done, but don't worry about them. You have to take care of yourself and really don't have much time to spend thinking second-rate thoughts.

Women should be capturing the "networking" approach and helping each other climb the ladder. This is absolutely necessary. Many do not subscribe to this idea and are hurting the possibilities of capable women getting ahead. I recently read about a dynamic woman who worked her way to senior vice president. She was proud of this achievement because she had seven men reporting to her. She may see this as a great victory over men, but she isn't helping other women. Why isn't she demanding more women in her unit? Why isn't she networking?

Women hurt themselves when they view other women as threats because the other women may come close to doing a job as well as they do. Men will continue to have a distinct advantage if women claw their way to a higher position and forget to include other women for fear that they will be threatened by those same women. Women need allies and networking does achieve equality. Until women realize the need to appreciate women as well as men in those they supervise, they will be limited in their achievements.

SYNOPSIS

Born from an egocentric, domineering attitude that uses the theory, "You wash my back and I'll wash yours," to live by, the "Good Ol' Boy" system has played every game, performed every dirty trick, used everything and everyone to prevent women from being accepted as equals. It's not all their fault, however. They were taught by equally egocentric, domineering, dirty players, their male mentors. This selfish, dictatorial mindset was, and frequently still is, impenetrable and very uncharitable when a female challenger comes knocking at their door.

Some women have begun to penetrate this power base and declare a kind of war on it. It is being fueled by a change of attitudes, a strong message defining a new game plan and women's ability to persevere. Women have begun to change their thinking about their ingrained attitudes and have discarded negative attitudes. They are getting down to the business of knowing the real game plan and of adjusting when men purposely change the rules of the game. Women, too, have arrived at a new age of enlightenment.

There is little evidence that men alone will offer you an opportunity to equalize your differences. The "good ol' boy" system won't permit it. Men selfishly ignore the disadvantages women suffer and relish their superiority. To challenge the "good ol' boys" takes a strong woman. But you can be made to be strong if you learn to build strong character and shed your weaknesses. A strong character and determination surprises most men and can weaken their negative attitude toward you. If you are better prepared, you will gain recognition. If your performance is superior, you will win promotions.

Women must believe in themselves so that, as they enter the field of competition, they will be recognized as strong contenders with formidable natural resources and a more determined resolve. But each woman can't stand alone and win. Women need to work together and establish friendships and ties in order to pull each other upward in the workplace.

The world is full of people whose notion of
a satisfactory future is, in fact,
a return to the idealized past.
—Robert Davies

Conceit is God's gift to little men.
—Bruce Barton

First, women must want to succeed above all else, then they must work harder than anyone else and certainly much harder than any man. . . . She will be in for a rough fight, but it's worth it, especially if she ends up having six or seven men reporting to her.
—Linda Shear

8

The Learn-To-Know-What-Good-Is Theory

To help you overcome the one-sided advantage men have over women and to better balance the odds for your arrival and survival as an equal player as you challenge each other for the advantage in the workplace, I have developed some self-help tools. Some of these *he* knows, others are new. The "Learn-To-Know-What-Good-Is Theory" is one of the new self-help tools I have developed and used for many years. It is a contemporary approach to identifying and curing the ills of inferior work standards, production and complacency. It was a product of my latent desire to see women improve their work ethic to a much higher level than is normally present and to reach a level of excellence that would provide them with an edge as they compete with others in the workplace.

I have used this approach for twenty years in competing with literally hundreds of men and a few women in a very demanding, fast, competitive industry.

"Learning-To-Know-What-Good-Is" was born out of my necessity and desire to be better-than-average or best in those tasks or assignments of highest priority that were offered to me. I offer it to you as a rock solid approach in being the very best you can be and in positioning yourself mentally for the many situations in your career that will demand top performance. Before you can reach the level of knowing what "good" is, you must first be able to recognize "good" and be able to define it for others. This may sound sophomoric, but it is not. There are many different levels of "good," and there are different levels of excellence. Everyone judges excellence in his or her own way and with different parameters. To reach a high level of excellence, you must first be able to recognize what "good" is. A particular level of good to some is a level of excellence to others and vice versa.

This self-help tool, along with others, will be discussed further in this and subsequent chapters. These tools are fashioned for you, especially for you as a woman, and they are designed to insure your success.

The "good" theory will help you to better understand why it is easy for some to satisfy the boss and achieve high goals and standards while others work distressfully but fail because they don't recognize the real objective.

The purpose of this theory is to ultimately raise your standards and work quality to unlimited heights in order to proclaim you as the new pacesetter, the new level of excellence and the one whom all your peers try to emulate.

As I worked with people in general and attempted to satisfy the desires and goals established by my boss and other company executives, I found that many times I was not on the same page when it came to understanding what was really required when he said:

"I want your very best."

"It must be exceptional work."

"It will require an excellence level just to be acceptable."

When I didn't quite measure up after working hard, I went through a mental post-evaluation process to identify what went wrong and why he didn't accept my work. After all, I did achieve *my* "excellent" level. I finally realized, in establishing similar goals and in assigning tasks requiring a measurement of good, excellent, etc., that I wasn't always getting what I wanted from those who reported to me either. This proved to be very frustrating. How could I satisfy my boss when those working for me couldn't identify the real objective! The awakening I experienced needs to be repeated in many workplaces today. It is the communications link to good overall productivity. I want you to recognize it so that you will be a step ahead. I want you to learn it from my experience. *Learn the boss's standards and adopt them for yourself.*

Not too long after I was able to recognize what "good" is and finally found myself in tune with the boss, I was promoted to a much higher, prestige position as a district manager—responsible for $50-million-plus in sales and overseeing and mentoring over 1100 employees (95% women).

This lesson put me in touch with my abilities and gave me an understanding of how much work one can actually do and do well when given the opportunity, trust and confidence necessary for excellence. More than that, however, it opened my eyes to understanding why there was a problem with the "good" or "excellent" acceptance level that I had failed to recognize earlier and had often agonized over.

The Theory

When six or seven responsible people are given the same assignment with the same goal and the same set of parameters, they will not achieve the same results. Some will evaluate their performance only to find one or more of their peers had "blown them away." Although aware that they were better than average, they found they were still not good enough. Only one person really did it right and achieved the goal. This one person will go on to achieve an even higher level of excellence. From this chain of events a new phrase is born that states, "Someone will do it right—they always do." I want you to be that person.

How does that someone do it right?

To really understand the "good" theory, you must have an understanding of:

1) your boss's standards,
2) your subordinates' standards, and
3) your own standards.

For example, one day we were having a major inspection visit from "*the* boss," the C.E.O. As he and I walked the store and inspected practically every 5-foot section for display, overall appearance, sizing, and all other required concepts, I sometimes heard good comments and sometimes heard not-so-good ones. Of course, I thought everything was superb. After all, we had worked exceptionally hard, long into the night to prepare.

After the inspection was completed I asked the boss what he thought of the store, naturally expecting an outstanding rating. He replied, "Jack, it's okay but it's not really good. You can do better; you need to raise your standards even higher." Obviously this didn't sit well. I felt like I had been slammed to the mat by a wrestler. My ego took a real hit and it didn't take long for my associates to capture the lousy mood either.

I rebounded enough to politely ask, "If what we have done here isn't good enough, then where can I go to see with my own eyes what you really think good is?" He immediately directed me to another store he had inspected and invited me to go take some of my people and see what "good" was. We swallowed our pride and made the trip. He was right, and we all learned that what "good" is to one, is "not so good" to another, and that before you can measure up, you'd better know what the boss's standards of "good" are.

Once you have mastered the boss's method of evaluation and level of performance, you can work to raise those levels in your people. Once you achieve this with his/her blessing, you now know you are on the same page, playing the same tune and can satisfy the boss. Everyone now knows what "good" is and can begin to work to raise that standard. Your boss established it. You saw it, your employees adjusted to it—all that is left now is to maintain it and work toward improving it. When you improve on the boss's "good," you will soon be recognized as the pacesetter, the one everyone else comes to see, copy and emulate—and that is a very rewarding feeling. And the boss will love it.

With this in mind, you are now aware why a few people win and most lose, why some people achieve the competitive edge and some fall into a rut. You now know what "good" really is.

Putting the Theory to Work

To achieve your career goals and to do it in as short a time as possible, you will find "learning-to-know-what-good-is" a valuable tool in achieving success. Just because you are a totally committed career person who works like a slave on your job, puts in the maximum number of hours at work (not to mention mental work while off duty), this doesn't and won't insure your success. You have to know what *really* is expected so that you can plan and chart the shortest and most effective course to your goal. Once you know what the boss wants and what that level of "good" is, then you can proceed to raise your current level of "good" to your new level, establishing a higher level of excellence and raising yourself to the highest level in the group. Now your peers will have to work harder to reach you while you continue to work to raise your own level even higher. Sounds like a lot of work? It is! And that is why early on I warned you that a total commitment will be absolutely necessary in this career process.

If you want a track team to win the high jump, you find one person who can jump seven feet, not seven people who can jump one foot.

The one who jumped the seven feet established a level that the others will have to attempt to achieve. They now know what "good" is, what they are jumping for and what is expected of them.

However, more is still needed on your part.

Now that you have seen and understand "good," you will still not achieve the same results simply by recognizing it. You must, in fact, physically work the job, constantly improving the output to continually insure success while maintaining the course. You must plan and control the work and be involved if you want to receive your deserved results. The high jumper didn't achieve seven feet because she/he just knew how to do it. Success was achieved because she/he worked at it time and time again until she/he perfected a new height, the new level that others must now work toward.

In reaching this highest level, you rightfully become the pacesetter, the leader of your particular work group. It means others will look up to you and seek your help in teaching them how to achieve new heights. You will evolve into a "mentor/advisor." This is perhaps the greatest award. It is an exhilarating feeling when it happens and your self-confidence is now sky high.

You Have the Edge

Knowing you can do something better than anyone else is what achievement is all about.

You have learned what "good" really is and forever more you will never come up short against your peers when in a competitive battle. You have the edge. You are state-of-the-art.

This approach can be applied to anything you ever really want to do. To get the best grades in school, you first have to know what the teacher or system accepts as the top. Then find the ones who achieve and follow their lead.

If you want to be the one who gets promoted, you must first know what the goal is before you challenge it. You must then find out how others before you achieved this level. Then you must work very hard, with 100% commitment, to exceed their results.

This 100% commitment of course, means that you must eliminate all negative thoughts or maybes when going for your goal. You can't even allow a short cut or detour in your plan, for that will short circuit your total commitment. Thoughts that substitute your goal cannot be allowed, *i.e.,* "Well, if I don't make it, I can always do . . ."

I firmly believe in the "Learn-to-know-what-good-is" theory and I also believe you will find it most rewarding as you pass up all those "good ol' boys" on your way to a successful career.

A word of advice from one of the women I interviewed who has reached a director's position (on her way to vice president). This woman has lived it all and seen the rest when it comes to the treatment of women in the workplace. I asked her how she got where she is and what advice she thought would help women in the workplace today.

She said, "First, women must *want* to succeed above anything else; then, they must work much harder than anyone else and certainly much harder than any man. A woman has to be better prepared and have higher standards and a strong self-discipline. She will be in for a tough fight, but it's worth it, especially if she ends up having six or seven men reporting to her." This theory will help give you the edge.

SYNOPSIS

Simply put, the "Learn-to-Know-What-Good-Is" theory is the training of oneself to identify the objective, to recognize and emulate the boss's standards, to find out who is doing the best job and receiving the boss's recognition, and then to establish a disciplined goal and a commitment to set an even higher standard. Work this plan with the assistance of those around you and that new standard of excellence will be achieved.

You gain strength, courage and confidence by
every experience in which you really
stop to look fear in the face.
You are able to say to yourself,
"I have lived through this horror.
I can take the next thing that comes along."
You must do the thing you think you cannot do.
—Eleanor Roosevelt

9

Self-Confidence: If It Is to Be— It Is Up to Me

Women have been criticized excessively over the years for lack of self-confidence, self-esteem, enthusiasm and the courage to take risks, all qualities necessary to compete and compare equally with men. The lack of these ingredients is regarded to have ruined the progress of women in general and in the workplace. Our everyday media parade, *i.e.,* women's magazines, newspaper columns and television, especially talk shows, focuses on these inequities and rarely, if ever, offers helpful solutions. The media criticizes and condemns you deeper into despair. It is easy to "bitch" and complain about a situation, but this type of indulgence is useless. It will even turn you off, since the media never constructively offers any real answers—usually just raises the issues, or at best offers only the "pop culture" solution of the moment. At any rate, these missing qualities are often the target of opportunists who choose to take advantage of weakness by keeping you suppressed so they can implement their own ideas and feed their self-image. In this chapter, I will address self-confidence and the "If It Is to Be, It Is Up to Me" theory.

Women *do* tend to shy away from new tasks, new ideas and change. This is particularly true at lower levels of job categories; however, it also tends to carry over into higher levels as well. You take and maintain a negative posture because you are fearful of your ability to adjust to the unknown, but you must learn to accept new tasks and ideas confidently and take on a true challenge if you intend to move ahead in the workplace. Confidence is the most essential factor in carrying out a good performance and achieving goals.

Your negative approach in tackling new things is a result of fear of inadequacy. You have already gone through formative years in a learning process and you don't consider yourself capable of repeating the process. Sometimes you even belittle yourself into thinking you are incapable of learning new ideas and that you lack sufficient intelligence (self-confidence). You are fearful of failure, of risks you can't take because you fear that doing so can put you out the door. This fear, this self-belittlement, these negative thoughts have no foundation and will block the real "you" from success and full accomplishment. It is your lack of self-confidence that causes this attitude.

In my opinion, you take this position naturally because what you receive from these new ideas and changes are usually for the furtherance of someone else. Why should you knock yourself out? You don't see personal progress even if your work is best. All you see is that someone else (normally the male boss or even a male peer) will steal your ideas and walk away with all of the rewards. No wonder you and many women like you feel the same and just want to be left "as is" and remain somewhat disinterested or passive. All of this leads to complacency and repressed anger (not to mention long-term effects on your health), and your skeptics are quick to exploit this attitude.

I have observed this many times in the workplace and can offer you examples of extraordinary women who suffered these feelings while deep down inside they really shouted to be heard. In the numbers of women interviewed for this book, I heard a message of "What's the use?" I hear this repeated frequently in social gatherings as well. And, as I talked to women on various higher levels in the workplace, this same message was repeated and repeated and repeated.

However, as you move further upward, I find you no longer self-destruct but still hang on to some negativity, disbelieving that a change for the better may really have taken place. Complacency is obviously no longer the feeling, or you wouldn't have taken a few risks and advanced to a higher level of work. You still, however, may have a problem with self-esteem as you challenge your capabilities and feelings of belonging and acceptance. You may even still feel insecure as you go "head-to-head" in competition with men.

You sometimes continue your deep-rooted lack of self-confidence, even though you already are somewhat of an achiever. You still don't find yourself as enthusiastic or as excited toward the project goals as you see some of the men. Just when you need it the least, there is a tendency to let insecurity sneak its ugly influence into your character and destroy your motivation. These attitudes and reactions are understandable considering where you as a woman have been, what traditional stereotype training you have received, and the suitable influences and sufficient support you have lacked in helping and encouraging you to overcome these handicaps. No use dwelling on the past. It is the future that is important and it is time now to work on improving your self-confidence.

Self-Confidence Influences Success

I will further discuss self-confidence and the primary role it plays in your overall success and its importance in solving and carrying out solutions to the unique problems that come from being a woman—competing for respect. But let's first characterize what self-confidence is and how it influences your success.

When *she* enters a room, an office, a meeting, or any other gathering, her personal magnetism captures everyone's immediate attention. She may be extremely attractive to a point of distraction—but not necessarily.

She may possess an exquisitely trim figure—but not necessarily. Her coiffeur and dress may exude meticulously tasteful attention—but not necessarily.

All of these and more she can claim as positive possessions, but this still isn't what she is really about. Her real strength is her ability to capture immediate attention *because of her attitude*. People around her see this beauty every day and, while it may be intimidating to some, the message she sends is, "This is me; I know who I am, and I feel great about myself."

With her winsome smile, she captivates even the most skeptical audience. She speaks with direct eye-contact, making you feel special, and she never releases until she has made her point. Even though she may be nervous, it doesn't show. She is very positive and secure and knows where she is and why she is there. She is the epitome of self-confidence and a classic model to emulate.

Let me explain. I have just described a real woman—a vice president of an extremely large company. She recently was the main presenter at a seminar for over 300 sales people and sales managers—a rather large, informal gathering. This was her first in-house seminar with so many highly-educated, extroverted over-achievers (about 75% were men—the other

25% being women indicates some progress has been made in this company).

She enters this large meeting room cheerily and very business-like. She is an absolute carbon copy of the woman I described and more. With her captivating smile she grabs everyone's attention—even those who would rather hear a presentation from one of their own.

When she speaks, her eye contact is perfect (from practice) and she never releases the spell until she has captured her point. Yes, she is nervous, but it is not obvious.

She has taken complete charge and has riveted everyone's attention. She plays the role of authority well. She is, indeed, the epitome of self-confidence.

The mostly male audience, struck by her beauty, begins to size up this young woman and the whispers begin. Then they begin to titter and outdo each other with terse, "no class" remarks about her status—who she is, how she really got to be where she is, and so on. You know the lingo. I know you have heard it, because I have, in one form or another, hundreds of times.

Beforehand, they just couldn't wait for her presentation so they could exploit any miscues or make her feel uncomfortable. They hoped for a question-and-answer segment at the end so they could disarm her and pick her apart. It didn't happen. Her presentation and self-confidence disarmed them completely, leaving them frustrated and spellbound. She did have the question-and-answer period, but the "good ol' boy" group was so stunned by her excellence and fearful that she would outdo them, they could only comment on how great she was. But wouldn't you know? Someone did hear the comment, "She was really great—for a woman." *Men just don't get it.*

This macho crowd met its match and found that a woman can be just as sharp and intelligent as any man. I wish I could get her to bottle her presentation so it could be passed around.

One thing is certain, she is fearless, well-educated and well-versed in her career emphasis. She knows she has to be better than any man and she takes that extra step to get there. She really knows what "good" is.

This anecdote serves two purposes:

1. It is a perfect example of a woman who has learned and developed a strong self-confidence—both in her career and her personal life.

2. Her vice presidential status gives affirmation both to the commitment and the kind of success that can be achieved when women develop a strong self-confidence. No question, looks enhance, but her inner strength is what everyone saw that day. Appearance became incidental.

Self-confidence is a force that provides immeasurable inner strength, inspiration, positive thinking and stimulation for your enthusiasm and motivation. It is the force that keeps you "pumped up" and ready to take on challenges. It releases you from intimidation and fear of failure. It forces you to excel in all projects, goals, confrontations and games.

Self-confidence is vital, because it gives you a secure, uplifting, happy-to-be-alive feeling. It is absolutely necessary, because it convinces you of your known abilities while enabling you to reach down and come up with some new ones. The higher, the more influential, the more powerful you become, the more self-confidence you will build—making your presence, character and personality more awesome. Indeed, it is vital and paramount to success. Make a pledge to yourself right now to cast aside your negative female upbringing and tell yourself you can do anything you set your mind to—*and you can.*

To become a winner,
you must first believe yourself to be one
within the depths of your subconscious mind.
—David A. Gustafson

To the Young Women

Those of you too young to relate to the total frustration and mental anguish that comes from lack of self-confidence must begin now to take steps and establish protective devices to help you develop and improve your self-confidence to survive the many known and unknown negative attacks it is sure to receive. This book will help you but *you* will have to work at it. It begins with your commitment to improve.

"Easy for him to say all this stuff about achieving immeasurable inner strength, becoming inspired and developing a positive attitude, enthusiasm and motivation," you might say as you try desperately to measure yourself against these requirements and this extra work. "He isn't a woman and knows nothing about how I feel, especially after some guy destroys me. He was never on the receiving end of some of these putdowns, sarcastic looks and comments, sexual remarks and harassment, physical embarrassment, sneers, smears, glares and unwanted comments."

No, I am not a woman and don't pretend to be an authority on women, but I do care and have personally witnessed all of these denigrations, the character assassination, the confidence-destroying treatment, hundreds of times in all sorts of situations, leveled by men against women in the workplace. I found men sometimes deplorable, disgraceful, uncomplimentary and down-right obnoxious. I am embarrassed by their actions and apologize for them. I feel that most men need a re-education toward women. First of all, it is ludicrous to even be discussing women as unequal. It is disgraceful and shameful even to consider a woman as a minority. Minority to what—to whom? Sorry guys, I don't see it that way and you shouldn't either. I challenge you to change and to accept women as total creatures of God in the same way you visualize and accept men.

I had the privilege of working with thousands of women in the workplace. I observed all the above-listed travesties and more with a very apologetic sense. On the other hand, please know that there is a certain group of caring men who are on your side and they, too, abhor the actions of those men who molest in any way your body, mind or spirit. Yes, there really are some who care and, as one of those, I offer my help and expertise to any who will listen and follow the directions. I am really committed to helping you succeed and achieve equal status in the workplace. It is my earnest desire to see conditions for women improve so that my two daughters, two daughters-in-law, four granddaughters and other family members will likewise be able to capitalize on this improved status. I hope by reading and sensing my attitude that you are convinced of my sincerity toward your improvement and success.

If you don't measure up to what is required, you never can or will have sufficient self-confidence. YOU MUST CHANGE! If you don't measure up, but feel you can and will achieve a high level of self-confidence, then you have taken a giant step on your own behalf.

"If it is to be, it is up to me" is a learned philosophy that, if constantly applied, will keep you on the right track to success in any endeavor. It will remind you that pointing the finger at others and making excuses for your shortcomings and failures is not the real answer and will get you nowhere.

The phrase is like a confession. It humbles you, honestly displays your feelings, and gives you a solemn purpose, so that you can take charge of your life and cope with its many demands.

Remember the young man who jumped into the icy, cold Potomac River on a very cold, January 13, 1982, to save a young drowning woman after a tragic plane crash? All of the nice things people said to him and about him will never equal the inner rewards he received and probably continues to receive for his heroic actions. He frantically sought help from those around him and, after receiving none, finally realized that he was it. If she was to be saved, he had to do it—and now!

"If it is to be, it is up to me," had to be his only thought as he jumped to his potential death in an all-out struggle to save a life.

While this is an extreme example, it illustrates what self-confidence can do on the spot when urgency is needed. I *urge you* to commit to improving your own confidence. When you do, you will gain increased self-assurance as it brings repeated success and, in turn, increases your self-worth. Those around you will see your efforts and the rewards and likewise will begin to emulate you.

You do not inherit self-confidence. You do not acquire it with wealth, good looks or a nice disposition. These will sometimes help, but they are not the key ingredients. Self-confidence really begins with you alone and how you feel about yourself, what you want out of life and how much you will sacrifice to get it. But remember, after all the hard work, you will also be the one to benefit from it.

If you speak of God, speak of love.
If you speak of yourself, speak of love.
—St. Bernadine

You have to think of yourself as someone special. You *are* special. You are not like all of those other people. So, it stands to reason that you do not need to act like them. You need to be yourself, to like yourself and to be happy. You really need to believe in yourself and to believe that you can achieve anything and everything you really set out to do.

That's not all, either. You have to have a desire to do something special with your life—a plan, a goal, something to shoot for, something special to you. Do you want happiness? Do something really special and achieve the greatest heights possible on your own, and you will be a happy person—and this is itself a reward. That woman who believed she could be better than any man and became the number one in sales in the country is a classic example of a firm desire, a plan, a goal to make it happen and the confidence to earn it. Does this woman know she is different? You bet she does, and she loves the idea.

You will have to be tough, tougher than men, to succeed. You will need self-confidence to stand up to them. When they throw verbal slurs at you, you must throw them right back. You have to be faithful to yourself and like yourself. You must develop a confidence that says, "Get with me or get out of the way." You can do this. I am counting on you!

Begin by visualizing yourself as a winner—one not afraid to take charge, always ready and able to accept setbacks and rejection, and one whose only aim is to be the best.

Self-confidence is an attitude. If you want to gain it, begin by thinking good things about yourself and love yourself. Do this every day and every chance you get. Soon you will begin to accept yourself in a positive way, strengthened by your personal conviction that you are the best. Carry that feeling about yourself wherever you go. It will come through as a sign of strength. Soon others will see it and begin to believe in you and cheer you on.

Nothing builds self-confidence faster than recognition from your peers and associates or applause from your audience.

SYNOPSIS

If there is a key lesson for women to learn or relearn in this book it is definitely the learning and practice of self-confidence. This attitude of greatness, of being in complete control of oneself, of strength to achieve and of knowing you will win is the basis of gaining all that is good and equal in this new era for women.

This chapter is extremely important to women because it announces your weaknesses, not as a criticism, but as an attitude toward yourself that needs to have a major overhaul.

Much of your time must be devoted to nurturing and elevating the growth in this important ingredient to your overall personal and career success.

When things get tough or you suffer temporary setbacks, you cannot, as so many women have done, pull yourself into a shell and pretend you do not have the ability to overcome reverses. You must develop self-confidence to overcome them.

The example in this chapter of the woman who mastered self-confidence should inspire you to reach for success. She is real, but only another woman, one who is determined to let the world know through her self-confidence that she is indeed up to the task of addressing and leading a large group (of mostly men) with overpowering success and mastery.

Reread this chapter constantly because it will provide you with inner strength, inspiration, a positive attitude, a stimulation to your enthusiasm and motivation.

You better live your best and act your best and think your best today, for today is the sure preparation for tomorrow and all the other tomorrows that follow.
—Harriet Martineau

10

Managing Your Way to Self-Confidence: Setting and Achieving Goals

Step 1 — Planning Your Goals

Establishing goals in life is essential to building self-confidence. Goals are also necessary if you are to achieve any measure of success. I suggest you establish personal as well as career goals so you won't dwell on minor points and end up feeling unaccomplished and useless. One personal goal I found to be a total asset is a spiritual life goal. It's important because it helps keep you thinking straight, and it controls your quality of life and the integrity of your work.

In setting goals, think positively. You have to make your goals tough enough so that you will work hard, hence providing a stronger feeling of accomplishment when you achieve them. Follow these steps:

1. Write down your objective—the one goal that you really want to achieve. (*i.e.,* if you are in sales, your goal could be to increase your personal sales figures by 10% in the coming year. Use a dollar amount, if you prefer.)

2. Clearly define how you are to achieve that goal, *i.e.,* I will make 20% more customer phone calls or call on five more new accounts every week. The following illustration will help choose your path to your goal.

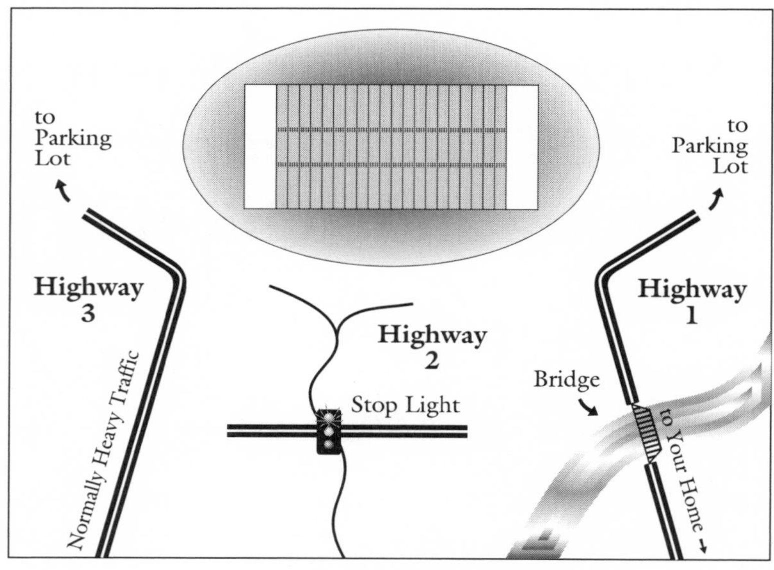

Option Map

To better insure success and eliminate the possibility that the one method you choose isn't the one that will doom you to failure rather than success, you should analyze and think of three or four different courses, options or roads to follow, any of which will insure your success. This way, you leave less to chance and eliminate as many road blocks as possible. In my lectures I have used this illustration and map to emphasize this important point. This mental exercise has the purpose of finding the right way to hold you to your committed goal and eliminate failure due to poor or inadequate planning. Keep in mind that you are only permitted to employ one option.

To see how this works, let's pretend you are going to the biggest football game of your college career and the stadium is out of town in the suburbs! See the Option Map.

Highway #1 is the closest to your home and closest to the gate you will enter, but the rain has not let up for a week and there is the possibility that the bridge may be closed due to high water by gametime.

Highway #2 will force you to go through town and is the longest route, meaning long delays at stop signs, red lights and so on. In addition, about a half mile from the stadium is a five-way intersection and one of the longest traffic signals in the state.

Highway #3 is a great highway, but it is known to always be bumper-to-bumper during peak times, such as before a game.

Hopefully, you now can visualize what is meant by clearly defining the various options you have as to how you will achieve your goal. This method is a mental exercise designed to sharpen your intellect and increase your ability to plan successfully. In this scenario, probably any highway would eventually get you to the football game. However, if you start out too late to go around the washed bridges (Highway 1) you might miss the entire game.

If you decide to take Highway #2, you chance a late arrival, perhaps missing the pregame activities or part of the first quarter, plus the fans who arrived early will not particularly like the interruption while you take your seat.

And what about Highway #3? Should you chance the bumper-to-bumper traffic and then possibly arrive and not find a place to park?

The mental rudiments you use when establishing how you will achieve your goal are the most important part of goal setting and must be given your fullest attention. All too often the goal process is just a verbal exercise that, if let stand, will sound great and produce nothing, because (1) there is no real commitment established and (2) no time has been taken to make sure that the right approach is chosen to ensure success.

Which of these highways is the right one to get to the stadium on time and achieve the goal? The answer lies in your own planning, but mostly it is a matter of timing and how early you start. Suffice it to say that a well-thought-out approach that takes into account all possibilities is the lesson.

3. Now that you have set the path to the goal, you must find a way to measure it. Failure to establish a checkpoint will automatically result in your straying from the goal or drifting, simply because you are not locked into a periodic reminder of what you said you were going to achieve. Goals must be measurable, with checkpoints every week, month and quarter.

This is a process that will help you achieve success in anything you truly desire. You must have self-discipline and you must really want to achieve that goal in order to find success.

Now you can plan the best and most expedient route to success.

Why do we select three or four roads or options? Once again, all roads will probably lead eventually to the goal, but by allowing yourself to go through this thought process, you are (1) convincing yourself of success, (2) building your self-confidence and (3) reinforcing your commitment by analyzing the best-suited approach. You are acting with a professionally-managed method of achieving results, and not just letting things happen. You are controlling what is happening.

This process works and is most successful in many major companies.

Nothing improves your self-confidence so much as an organized plan of attack. Once you become fully organized, you will be amazed at how much extra time you now have. I once worked for a company president who had first-hand knowledge of almost any task that took place in the company at any single time. He not only knew "what good is," but he was an outstanding example and exponent of the "Learn-to-know-what-good-is" theory.

One day I asked him how he was able to know and remember so much at one time and how he was so knowledgeable about even the smallest details. He said, "You have to be well-organized. You have to have good people working for you and you have to delegate. But mostly, you have to be organized." He used a goal-setting process religiously and was convinced it was essential.

- Once you get organized, you will be better able to visualize your goals and the need to achieve them. You create self-confidence. You can clearly establish worthwhile objectives, making certain you are serious about the results and the benefits.
- Make goals, not New Year's resolutions. This process works for career and personal life goals alike.
- When selecting the required results, feel comfortable that they are reachable; not too easily, yet with enough demand to cause you to work.
- To be successful, goals must be written and kept close at hand where you can see them and can be continuously aware of them. They must be measurable so you can see achievement along the way (use dates, times, amounts).
- Dates must be established in your written goals so you can check your progress, goal accuracy and make possible adjustments. Adjust your goal checkpoints, etc., if circumstances change or the original goal has lost its value.

Whenever possible, career goals should be made in conjunction with the goals of your associates and subordinates. The quantitative results of your goal should be an accumulation of the quantitative results of those reporting to you. With this approach, you have a better chance of achievement. All you have to do is keep others motivated.

It is often said that when men achieve something worthwhile, they first celebrate, then go on immediately to attack the next mountain.

Women, on the other hand, having worked hard and achieved a worthwhile goal, too often spend time reliving and reviewing their success—then try to re-evaluate and study how they could have done it better. Consequently, they lose time getting started on the next mountain, creating a stressful catch-up situation as they see their male peers off and running. Don't do this! Set the goal, achieve the goal, celebrate briefly and get on with the program. You can't beat a very competitive man unless you accelerate your thinking and develop a personal sense of urgency.

Step 2 — Working Your Plan

It is absolutely essential to plan your goals and then to work your plan if you want to be successful. First, establish the desired results:

What is the starting date?

How exactly will you begin? What is the first step?

What tools will you need along the way?

Do you have to contact anyone for additional input so you can intelligently establish an accurate goal?

How will you monitor progress?

How much time do you need?

As you create your plan, you will begin to feel more comfortable, more professional and even more powerful by knowing you are doing this in an organized way.

You may want to test your process on a smaller scale first. Choose something like losing weight so you can feel better. By learning and applying the thought process described earlier, you can easily proceed. Do you want to begin a walking or jogging program? How about an aerobics class or health club? This approach will work and you will build self-confidence with each step. You may even lose weight. Make sure your plan is workable and that it can easily fit into your routine, i.e., don't attempt to join a health club 25 miles away. If you do, you will be planning failure because you will probably dream up a multitude of reasons why you can't get there.

Planning is a discipline, something that requires perseverance. Self-discipline and self-confidence are inseparable and will keep you focused on results. A strong self-discipline is envied by most, especially those who go through life willy-nilly. If you hear someone criticize self-discipline, it is because they are jealously lazy. If you are young and just starting out in a working environment, or thinking about a career and what you will do with your life, it is in your best interests to follow this lead as it relates to planning and organizing. It will help you and help build your self-confidence.

First, you will need to decide on a higher education. A college education or equivalent is absolutely essential. Begin immediately—don't procrastinate. Men do that. Set a completion date so you can really get down to career business. Try to pick up a mentor along the way so you will have hands-on guidance. Seek out someone who will guide you. Don't be afraid to ask a man (or woman) for help. Be bullish and forward. Make this new ally a partner to your thinking. He/she may surprise you and go above and beyond your expectations for help. Many men are willing to help a woman succeed. Not all men belong to the "good ol' boys" dynasty. Take advantage of this help and support. Grab it and run. You need all the help you can get.

If you have already moved upward in job status and have established a career path and completed your higher education, you are fortunate. Are you in a quandary as to what to do next? Does your career meet your expectations? If not, it may be time to adjust your plan and re-think your career path. This quandary is more common than you think, so don't despair. After considerable study and weighing, you may find comfort and peace of mind if you change careers completely. It's better to start over than to continue in a rut. Read what a frog has to say about a rut.

> Two frogs were hopping down the road on their way to the local pond for an afternoon swim. On the way, they came upon a friend who occupied a rut in the road. They encouraged their friend to join them for a swim, but he said, "I am stuck in this rut and can't get out. No matter how hard I try, I can't jump high enough to make it out of this rut."
>
> The friends, realizing they could do nothing to help, went on their way. Once they reached their swimming pond, they turned around to see their friend close behind. They asked him how he had gotten out of the rut.
>
> "Did something fall in and allow you to climb out?"
>
> With a simple reply he said, "No one helped me and nothing fell into the rut. I looked down the road and saw a truck coming!"

Things got really urgent, so he was forced to find enough strength to jump, and that is the way we often deal with life's problems. Crisis situations can be eliminated by good pre-planning. Don't dilly-dally in a go-nowhere job and waste time stuck in a rut when changing your career goal is urgently necessary. Don't wait for a truck to come down the road.

If you are just making an adjustment in your career, don't be afraid to make the change. Even a job change could make sense. A job change enlivens your thinking and purpose and broadens your horizons. Also, it is the right thing to do to keep you from getting parked in a nowhere job. Job changes are good for your income as most result in higher pay and greater rewards—the kind you can spend. More than anything, you must strive to be happy, to feel the rewards of accomplishment and know that you are contributing to your success. Don't waste time waiting for the boss's promises to materialize while he promotes his cronies to your well-earned position. As you gather good working credentials, enlist the aid of a good professional recruiter. These often do a much better job than you can when seeking change.

As you move forward, don't forget to tell yourself how great you are! You are, you know, or you wouldn't be progressing. Pat yourself on the back. Most of the time you probably will be the only one who will. Most companies fail to recognize the value of positive reinforcement and its profitable rewards of increased productivity. Be happy with yourself, be patient with your progress in these changes and remember that some changes take longer than others.

Heighten Your Status; Increase Your Worth

Planning at the advanced level needs to be even more precise. You are already an achiever—maybe even an over-achiever. Time spent in your present position determines what happens next. Don't stay stuck too long. You are worth something now, both to your employer and to yourself. You may be worth more to another employer. Don't overlook that option.

Your career goals should be projected from one to three years ahead. Does your present situation look promising? Talk to those who make the decisions. If your boss doesn't know, ask permission to talk to his boss or with any individual who knows. This is no time to be shy and introverted. It may take a lot of courage—but do it. Most men will. You must also. Get pushy! It's time to be that squeaky wheel.

You know by now through the grapevine what future positions are available to you. Give considerable attention to selecting this next move because you are now fine-tuning your life's career. Make sure all of those above you know what you have in mind. If you want a specific job, tell them so. This is important, because now you should be totally committed and fully motivated toward goal achievement—and with more than enough self-confidence to go forward and succeed.

If you are ready to turn on the steam and you don't want to waste energy and time going nowhere, seek guidance and ask the opinions of those higher than you. Study their suggestions. Gather more information, if necessary, so you have a full understanding of the big picture and the necessary information to make a quality decision.

As you progress upward, you will easily see the rewards of planning and working your plan. You can also feel the strengths you have gained by self-confidence and you now have the savvy to continue your upward movement more comfortably. This is a fabulous feeling, one you would like to shout about. Do so, and make sure you tell your boss of your successes. Keep his boss tuned in to your progress also.

Step 3 — Staying on Course

Continually work with your goals. Always know where you are. Keep them in big print at your work station. Put another copy in your car and one on the refrigerator at home. Don't let that "out of sight, out of mind" thief steal your success. Constant review will keep you working hard, or at least jog you into remedial action. By staying on course, you are increasing your sense of self-worth, self-esteem and self-confidence.

You will suffer occasional setbacks (no one is perfect); just get back on the course quickly and move on. Don't dwell on them, and try to establish what went wrong. A negative attitude will put you in park and may even cause you to self-destruct. Women may become overly-sensitive to reversals and take them personally even though they are not at fault.

You will show great character if you bounce back with a positive attitude and get on with it. Your people will cheer and rally around you.

Again we are talking about self-discipline. It sometimes takes a full measure of the stuff to stay the course. It's easy to procrastinate or turn to short or long term excuses, especially when the pressure is on. Likewise, stress and pressure can cause you to change your route to your goal without the necessary redefining and adjustment. Don't let frustration lead you.

Another time that might tempt you to change course is during holidays or post-holidays when laziness occurs. The same can happen during vacation and post-vacation times. Put your self-discipline into high gear now in order to throw off these nasty beasts. Constantly petition yourself to be vigilant and on guard against interruptions and outside influences by well-intentioned associates, family members or caring men in your life. They can stifle your judgment and scuttle your purpose and resolve. Those women who have achieved success have established safeguards against these dangers. You have to know when and how to play but also when to turn it off and get serious.

Laziness is the real enemy of us all. Unfortunately, we are all tempted and have to suffer with it. Those who fall victim will never see success. Put up your guard. Ask yourself, "What am I here for?" Be reminded that success is what you are after. Nothing less is your goal, and you can get there from here because you are a woman.

Step 4 — Accumulating Successes

As you move closer and closer to achieving your goal, you will gain more and more self-confidence. You now understand how those successful women we spoke of in earlier chapters had the strength and stamina to succeed.

Real self-confidence starts when you begin your early and smaller successes. These provide the groundwork toward further achievement and prove how valuable and necessary self-confidence can be.

Earlier, I talked about how men achieve self-confidence by playing sports and boy games. They learn how to lose as well as win. People tend to learn more from losing. Losing can have a very positive influence on good career growth. As men fine tune this winning-losing process, they eventually (if they become successful in career advancement) learn to play the game so well that losing becomes rare. If it does occur, it is just *not acceptable.*

At any rate, they gain more confidence and this explains why some men develop such egocentricity and why those at the top exude such strong self-confidence and oversized (and sometimes overbearing) egos.

This is not necessarily a criticism of men as much as it is a natural result of success. It happens to women as well. I hope it will happen to you. But, unfortunately, you have fewer role models to emulate, so you have to go it, more or less, alone. No doubt most of you will handle it adroitly.

With success comes rewards and awards either monetary, verbal or both, and these are important to your future self-confidence. Many people feel that money is not the only thing they seek to motivate them. I suggest that it be at least a close second. While high fives for a well-performed job is a valuable and powerful force to propel you into a positive human dynamo searching for more of the same, money is the real thing that measures your achievements and makes it possible to live the good life. Don't work for peanuts, and make very sure you are paid what *he* is paid. It's the law!

Positive reinforcement is an absolute must in today's workplace. However, it must be offered sincerely, with no predetermination. We have witnessed entirely too much verbal, negative destruction from the mouths of abrasive, so-called leaders. Words that hurt and ridicule destroy motivation, self-confidence, the individual, and the team. Don't be a part of it—it doesn't work and it will destroy *your* self-confidence and ability to lead. "Pretty please and thank you" still gets the job done.

The more positive reinforcement you spread around, the faster your team players will work, the quicker they will respond, the happier they will be and the faster you will become Number One. This point is so important that it is repeated in a number of chapters in this book.

You have reached your goal! Now it's time to reward your people with thanks. Thank them in a group setting. Go one-on-one with those who gave more or were outstanding. Do this always, keeping in mind that you are nothing without their good work and loyalty.

The act of positive reward also rewards you with a great inner feeling of self-love, self-esteem and further self-confidence. It's exhilarating and lasting. This feeling also manifests itself in that love I talked about earlier. These platonic love affairs between you and your associates can only result in greatness.

Now that you have set goals, know the rewards and have achieved self-confidence, let me tell you that you are the greatest!

SYNOPSIS

It is frequently stated that if you create a goal without a plan, a course to follow, that any road will eventually lead you to the goal. In this highly-competitive world and with women beginning to make forward strides into the male-dominated workplace, exemplary work, strict attention to detail and precise, well-thought-out planning is absolutely essential. The haphazardness of the mind that formulates a poor plan or no plan must be left to the apathetic male. To merely take just any road or process to achieve your important goals is not the way to seize your destiny.

Companies either succeed or fail because of their goal processes. Companies as well as their key important associates will not survive without looking into the future, deciding what success they desire for themselves and their company or unit and preparing a well-defined, professional way to proceed.

A structured approach to performing work is the right way to reach success. It is also a positive method of achieving an abundance of self-confidence. When you know where you are going and how you are going to get there, you can't help but feel good about yourself and your career success.

I have used this goal process for over twenty years with continued successes and increased paychecks. It worked for me continuously. There were times I had as many as fifteen measurable goals that I worked on simultaneously. There is no better way to win the battle of goals and goal setting than the one prescribed here.

Learn to obey before you command.
—Solon

Let the rewards of success, never the risk of failure,
take the leadership role in your life.
—Anonymous

Sow a thought, reap an act; sow an act, reap a habit; sow a habit, reap a character; sow a character, reap a destiny.
—Anonymous

11

Empowerment = Positive Thinking

Oh! The power of positive thinking! How necessary this is for achieving success. It transcends all negative influences and elevates your will to drive your energies and desires toward achievement. It is the basic influence necessary for the development of genuine enthusiasm. It helps one rise above adversity. It empowers the mind to prevail over raging pessimism, those who resist change, those who preach doom and predict disaster, and those who vilify success and achievement, and hinder progressive thought. It gives strength to repel trouble that could derail progressiveness and new ideas.

Positive thinking moves you to demonstrate mental and spiritual strength in managing and directing associates. It is automatically manifested in your everyday verbal contacts and is quick to be noticed by an aggressive superior or leader. To have it is to place yourself measurably above those who vacillate or who are stagnant, down-in-the-mouth pessimists. It dissolves anti-public thinking toward positive projects, growth and change. Positive thinking is the prime requisite in solving people's problems in the workplace and in everyday life. It is, without question, very necessary to a happy, warm, strong, purposeful and triumphant personal philosophy. You can't live without it and be successful. Cultivate it and it will reward you with additional self-confidence and happiness. Stay on course on this one; it is most essential. Promote positive thinking always; it will help build a successful, happy team.

Further, it is necessary to develop positive thinking to help offset negative day-to-day influences and ideas and to keep you from falling victim to a programmed guilt feeling that is continually reinforce by images in the media, particularly the press and television. They sensationalize pitiful and horrible personal tragedies to gain improved ratings and disguise their intentions as constitutional rights.

Recently on television news at 6:00, the television crew characterized the top five news subjects (which were already, by nature, mind destroying) in such a way as to leave the viewer with a feeling of self-blame and personal self-doubt. It ridiculed the disciplined approach, played up sensationalism to downside your mood and over-emphasized the trials and tribulations of the recipients of misfortune, leaving the viewer feeling completely dismayed, guilty and virtually distraught. The point is, if you are to maintain a positive attitude and good thoughts, you must not listen to, watch or read the news stories as presented. For this very reason, many people today refuse to read front page newspaper stories or watch news broadcasts on television. There are too many other good things to watch and read. Fortunately, there are a few networks which still can present news stories without the dramatics of negativism—and which will not put you into a world of hurt.

A Positive Affirmation

Earlier, I directed you to surround yourself with good people. It is also in your best interest to surround yourself with an abundance of positive thinkers as well. To achieve quality goals requires quality thinking. It is impossible to achieve success with "down-in-the-mouth" naysayers who delight in finding the worst in everything. Fill your mind with positive meditations and reflections and train it to quickly take a negative offering and turn it into a positive affirmation.

As a very positive reference, Henry Ford has been quoted as saying, "Your best friend is he or she who brings out the best in you. Always associate with the best." So, too, associating with positive-thinking people will promote the best in you. We are constantly influenced by those around us.

Among the rewards of positive thinking is the ability to keep a good mood. Positive-thinking people are generally characterized as smiling, able to find the good in people, see the good side of everything, and genuinely feel comfortable whether in a group, crowd, or all alone. They have built an inner guard against stress and are seldom seen going to the doctor for emotional distresses, pills and drugs.

Because positive people live on the high side, they are more in tune with problem solving and clear thinking. Consequently, they are better equipped to lead and mentor subordinates. Then, too, they are quick to identify rejection and position themselves against it. When things get nasty, they tend to keep a cool head while others lose theirs. This enables them to see things clearly, as they really are, and to make quality decisions. It is this strength that promotes additional logical, common sense solutions. It is this strength, too, that feeds the fires of self-confidence within and provides the impetus to lead.

If you are to win in this game and overcome that stereotypical stigmatism of being judged second-rate, incapable, or a mental weakling, you must develop an eagerness for an enthusiastic mindset. Positive thinking will empower you toward that end. You can develop a positive attitude by practicing the points outlined in this chapter. I urge you to begin now, because I am positive you will succeed!

Make this chapter your positive affirmation to change and promote positive thinking, not only in the workplace, but with anyone you meet. Your outlook on life will drastically change for the better, and loving yourself and those around you will become much easier, for it is really love that opens the doors of the heart for worthwhile passage.

SYNOPSIS

Positive thinking is like the electricity that turns on your microwave, T.V. or light bulbs. It is likened to this force because of the enormous power and influence it has over your thinking and subsequent actions. This power and influence moves you to demonstrate true thinking, the kind that motivates and inspires subordinates to seek and work in the right mental state. This creates a strong workplace with happy faces and quality workers.

The positive thinker is automatically better equipped to lead, because he or she is continually in tune with the project at hand and incapable of creating an apathetic or uncaring work atmosphere.

When you are empowered with positive thinking, you will be totally equipped to identify and repel rejection, promote logical and common sense solutions and develop an even stronger self-confidence.

Be masters of your petty annoyances and conserve
your energies for the big worthwhile things.
It isn't the mountain ahead that wears you out . . .
it's the grain of sand in your shoe.
—Robert Service

12

Enthusiasm—It Makes People Strong

If you have developed a positive attitude in the day-to-day interplay of give and take, you will receive more wins than losses. You will still have disappointments, frustrations and some second thoughts. How you deal with these is very important. These may bother you or even stymie your will to go on. *Get out of that mood.* You can't win with them—you can only continue to lose and destroy your spirit.

Remember, nobody wins all of the time. Learn from your failures in order to improve and avoid making the same mistakes later. Learn from your failures, because they are your best teachers. Winners don't dwell on losing, only on coming in first.

Successful people win and lose because they are totally involved in working toward their goals or company objectives. Lesser people always see things as "okay," because that is their quality level and standard. If you want to win, you must have enthusiasm and desire and be able to envision only the highest standards and work ethic on a continual day in, day out basis. Let up, and that man will run by you, run through you or run over you on his way to *your* goal.

Shun the propaganda that says men have more stamina and physical strength to achieve goals. Nonsense! Women are as tough and can match strength with any man. They also have strong endurance, not to mention more to gain. You must adopt the attitude that if this job is going to get done properly and on time—let a woman do it.

By now, I hope you have become "pumped up," are accepting the challenge or are at least feeling more positive about your strengths. Enthusiasm for the quality things in life is worth working for. "Lively interest," as it's sometimes called, is a challenge to indifference, which indeed is one of the frustrating enemies of women. Enthusiasm is the product of *self-confidence*. It arrives with an effervescence that can send you into an inspired frenzy and, if corralled and controlled, can move you to enlightened success and heavenly euphoria.

J.Fred Knott, an enthusiast who presided over a number of retail food companies and who later became a consultant to a renowned plaza and mall developer and also an instructor at Youngstown State University in Youngstown, Ohio, said:

> Enthusiasm makes people strong. It wakes them up, brings out their latent powers, keeps up incessant action, impels to tasks requiring strength, and these develop it. Many are born to be giants, yet few grow above the common man from lack of enthusiasm. They need waking up! If set on fire by some eager impulse, inspired by some grand resolve, they would soon rise head and shoulders above their peers. But they sleep, doze, wait for public sentiment, cling to the beaten paths, dread sacrifices, shun hardships, and die weaklings.

This superb message should be emblazoned in memory as a tool to work and live by. Our labors never become a reality, deadlines are never met, nothing really gets sold, the job doesn't get done properly without the *enthusiasm of the doer*. Then there are those who for one reason or another, even with a sincere desire for success, fail to ignite their inner strength with enthusiasm. Women can't afford to fall into this group. Women must develop a self-confidence strong enough to permit their enthusiasm to explode and lift them emotionally and spiritually to a higher level and beyond their wildest dreams. Enthusiasm makes things happen, fulfills dreams and develops dynamic leaders.

Enthusiasm is epitomized in sports both by women and men. It enthralls their spirit and gives them impetus to "hustle" in competition.

One who owns an abundance of it is sometimes called an "over-achiever." An "over-achiever" is nothing more than an extremely enthusiastic person who establishes and sets higher standards and achieves greater goals than others. They are normal humans who have developed stronger skills through stronger desires (enthusiasm). They want to do it; enthusiasm gets them there. They also learned what "good" really is.

The people who set the higher standards in the workplace and continually reach their goals, likewise are propelled to action by *enthusiasm*. It is a mindset that can be developed by submitting totally to the wants and desires of a group, division, region, company or self for the sole purpose of overall success. If you are sparked with enthusiasm, you can take charge and lead the team, division, region or, eventually, the company. Without it, you will "cling to the beaten path," shun leadership and eventually lose to your male peers.

Genuine enthusiasm has to come from the heart. It has to be nurtured and allowed to grow. Its negative enemies must be beaten down and not allowed to enter your mind. Reread the words of J.Fred Knott and be governed by his skillful references to the strength that is inspired by enthusiasm. Become a woman who inspires strong will, endless endurance and a genuine resolve to seek out and find the best. Train and mentor those who also seek a rewarding life and career, possess unwavering self-discipline and the ability and courage to hold to it and demand it from others. It is rather obvious that we need better leadership in the most important jobs in the country. I know it can come from women like you. I hope you will become the giant I think you are. You can if you develop and exercise strong enthusiasm.

The giants of yesteryear were those who would accept only the very best from anyone. "Do it over," was their code when work wasn't exemplary. "Do it over again," was their higher code if they sought perfection. "Take pride in your life and work," was their every day religion. They subscribed to none other. As a testament and monument to their enthusiasm and excellent work, their names are inscribed on walls of long-existing companies, in the sports halls of fame, and in the annals of medicine, education, religion and industry. You just can't beat those of high standards and you just can't be someone less if you, as a woman, are to excel.

SYNOPSIS

Whether or not you win at anything is simply dependent upon your will and desire to succeed against all odds. If you think positively and never let negative attitudes infiltrate your resolve or destroy your commitment, you can achieve a strong base for success. If you demand of yourself never to let frustration, disappointment or an occasional setback destroy your will, you will have developed an enthusiastic belief in yourself that will be hard for anyone to penetrate or defeat. Enthusiasm does indeed "make people strong," and it will keep you strong if you protect it.

If your boss fails to recognize your good work because you are a woman, then go around him. Don't accept second-class treatment.
—Jack McAllen

13

True Love Never Runs Smoothly— Neither Does Your Job

If you can't seem to get the hang of it or can't really get "turned on" in your career, then it could be that you are playing the wrong game or are on the wrong team. You could, however, be playing the right game on the wrong team. Think about this. It may be time to open a dialogue with your boss or company counselor. You may seek advise from someone from Human Resources within your own company, as they are generally trained to help you put things in order.

It could also be that now, having a definite, positive plan, you are vacillating in your career or have been bottled-up in a non-stimulating, boring job function. Remember, some man will pigeonhole you into a job slot either because you have become so good and so valuable—meaning, of course, that he is too lazy to move you up and retrain another, or he has stereotyped you to a point that includes your inability to function because you are a woman, or it's not a woman's company or some other self-serving excuse.

I have seen and witnessed many outrageous excuses and lies that men create to stymie women's promotions, but I really cringe when I think about the women who have been stuck in a tough, lower management position for years, simply because the boss or a succession of bosses actually blocks their promotions because these women are so very good in these jobs and most probably won't complain if they are passed over for promotion. It's ridiculous to see women working themselves into stagnation. You can change this by demanding to be heard and demanding to be treated fairly and equally. You will have to get tough-minded and apply the "work from strength" approach.

If your boss fails to recognize your good work because you are a woman, or fails to promote you because you are a woman, then go around him. Again, work from strength. It's your life, your career and your income that you are being cheated out of. You have the inner strength; just reach down for it. Do everything in your power to get personal satisfaction. Don't accept second-class treatment.

Don't Accept Poor Treatment

If you don't get the satisfaction you deserve and your superiors refuse to listen after you have tried every means, then go to the Federal Government and report them for violations of the Civil Rights Act and its 1991 amendment. More and more women are doing this today. You might fear this approach but, having done it, you will definitely feel better. I will go into this procedure in detail in the final chapters, when covering the E.E.O.C. and related issues. One thing to remember, reasonable attorney's fees are now provided for in the new civil rights act.

All of this requires a strong will and tenacity. If you fear reprisals, and if the openness and/or family-friendly attitude is not evident in your workplace, then you should seek outside advice from a talented, experienced counselor. There are many people, men and women, who will help you, and it doesn't have to cost a cent. Many government agencies as well as academic guidance counselors offer this help. Remember, retaliation against you is against the law.

Do not discuss your unhappiness or unfair treatment with your peers, people who report to you or other subordinates. This can be, and usually is, dangerous. There is an old and true axiom in business that says, "Always complain up—not down." The ones who have the power to help are those of higher authority and you will only add to the woes and burden the attitudes of subordinates if they see you upset. They also are not equipped to advise you and have a tendency to pass your problems on to other unsuspecting employees. Need I tell what the story will sound like when it finally reaches the end? When complaining up, make absolutely certain that you are right and have facts or evidence to prove it. Your credibility is on the line and you can't afford to damage it.

This mistake is made far too often by unsuspecting women, who trust too much in their feelings and instincts without considering the consequences. It has even ruined many good careers. Don't let this warning deter you, however. If you know you have a case, go for it.

I urge you also to be careful when confronting your well-intentioned husband or boyfriend with your workplace problems. They generally do have your best interest at heart and hate to see you upset, especially if you break down in tears. Experience tells me and now you, that they will overreact on your behalf and, among other things, will suggest or even demand that you quit. This may eventually happen, but it shouldn't be helped along by an irrational act. It isn't something you need when you are trying to solve serious job problems and when you are attempting to determine your career position and studying the options. Your significant other is a man, and most men do not like to see women unhappy. In addition, he surely does not want to feel that same unhappiness. This is not a criticism. It's a normal male reaction.

If things go wrong at work and you go home and "dump" on him, his first reaction may not be in your best interest. It may even cause a conflict. He will jump to your side in your defense. The question is, aren't you really capable of making decisions without him? The answer is—yes, you are. Make him a partner *after* you have reached a logical, common sense solution. Seek his help *after* you have studied all of the issues. Then, offer your thinking and position. At that point, you may like his answer better and he will treat you in a less stereotypical way.

If something is worth doing, then it's worth all of your effort. If it is worth doing, then you should become "gung-ho" and move positively, with confidence and enthusiasm to develop and lead the change to finality. A man will give most things his best effort, but if a man really latches onto something he feels strongly about, he will devote his all to the cause and stick with it until he wins. You must approach everything with the same "gusto" and with equal strength of purpose.

Self-confidence, positive-thinking, enthusiasm—these are the keys to achieving success. With this combination, plus hard work and a measure of good luck, you can't lose. The rewards can be great. And luck does have a heavy hand in it.

Abe Lincoln once said, "I am a great believer in luck, and I find the harder I work, the more I have of it."

J. Fred Knott said, "I was always the luckiest when I was working the hardest."

SYNOPSIS

Human nature has made it easy, maybe too easy, to dwell on the negative. It seems to settle in today's workplace and is fueled by those who have unhappy experiences with superiors and associates on a day-to-day basis. It is further fueled by the abrasive action of an unpredictable boss who seems to appear just in time to challenge your self-confidence, positive thinking, enthusiasm and your other positive armament with his admonition that yesterday's hard work and seemingly total effort did not meet with his standards, leaving you with a "What's the use?" attitude.

Rise above this criticism. Use good common sense and fair judgment to determine if he is right or wrong. Now let your enthusiasm, positive thinking, self-confidence and will to succeed kick in to put you above all of this and get you back on track. Believe in yourself! Don't forget who you are and what you are here for. There is much to learn from the times when your job doesn't run smoothly.

A tough lesson in life that one has to learn is that not everybody wishes you well.
—Dan Rather

Whenever you can, hang around the lucky.
—Jewish proverb

Don't take what they give you;
take what you want!
—Anonymous

14

Men Have the Power—Women Have the Purpose

We rarely see ourselves as we really appear to others. Sometimes a tone of voice, a gesture, a look, a smile, no smile or other body language can go a long way toward sending mixed signals, when in reality they are unintended and have no special meaning. When misread, they may misrepresent your actual thoughts. Similarly, some body language can be misinterpreted to have a special meaning. Men (and women) want you to be feminine, but not seductive, in the workplace. You must maintain femininity. In this chapter, we will discuss these characteristics so we can improve your overall image. If your seductive influences win out, then you had better re-evaluate your commitment, because it is in jeopardy.

While misinterpreted body language can be a fault or a habit, there are sure to be other characteristics that need improvement in order to perfect your image. For example, you may not be grammatically correct or well-experienced in the use of English. Your spelling may be poor or you may need to work on your vocabulary. You may need to improve your physical appearance, a fault that better eating habits or an exercise program may help to correct. There may be nested in your personality a temper problem, finding you sometimes too quick on the trigger and too soon to go for the jugular in a close encounter. Unfortunately, these are faults of many good, well-meaning people.

Another serious problem is that you simply may be suffering from lack of sleep for some reason and find it difficult getting up in the morning. If this is a lazy habit and you find yourself too frequently on the wrong side of the clock on arrival at work, then you must take control. This habit exhibits a lack of self-discipline and destroys many promising careers before they get started and most assuredly affects the careers of some very talented people. It can quickly mess up a good work history.

To be sure, you may have other weaknesses, faults or idiosyncrasies that come to mind or that you know or feel need to be corrected. I am sure we agree that some corrective action in the area of self-improvement needs to be taken by each of us.

Earlier, we engaged in a goal-setting process. Now is a good time to practice setting goals for improving yourself and your habits, so that when the time comes to set other personal and career goals, you have some experience with the process and thus a better chance to do an outstanding job. This, too, will lift your self-confidence and give you a more secure feeling, knowing that you already have some experience with the process.

How you feel, how you look and how you interface with people will have a great influence on your career life. Experienced executives and management people can be quick to judge and react favorably when you display a positive feeling about yourself. Your self-esteem does come through.

Women become more of a target than men where physical appearance and mental acumen are concerned. Unfortunately, as we discussed earlier, most men focus on your physical appearance before concentrating on your more pertinent mental qualities. This is very basic and something you have dealt with forever—it has been going on for over four million years.

It's Time to Take a Stand

As I read more and more about the rash of problems you are experiencing and witness the vivid portrayal on television and radio of the blatant mistreatment of women, I can only applaud you for your new-found courage to lash out at such perpetrators in your attempt to make things right for yourself. You have come front and center and dared to challenge those who misuse or misrepresent you. You have gone head-to-head with those who misjudge your attempts to communicate, seek acceptance, be friendly, or just plain act like an equal human being.

General Colin Powell recently got right to the point as he emphasized his position as a minority as he said, "If you are going to beat me—you'll have to beat me in my face." The mechanism for change is in place. Some political and social players are on stage in this power play who have the ultimate goal to eliminate the word "minority" when evaluating, communicating, interfacing or referring to women in any setting. Some men have always viewed women as "objects." These ideas have been passed on to them through the ages. It is a weakness, but one whose end may be in sight. Men (and women) are more educated today and the time has come to remove the stigma by making men realize their infractions against their equal partners on this planet. A rebirth of women's presence is now openly manifesting itself in every office, factory, retail establishment, technical firm and government facility.

Physical appearance is important to women. Properly presented, it enhances that important first impression. It's an advantage that characterizes a woman as having great self-esteem and self-love. Is it important? You bet it is! And it will always be. On the other hand, appearance is an equally important characteristic for men's acceptance by men as well. Attractive women are continually praised for their beauty by the boss or other men of influence. Accept it as a meaningful first impression and a male reaction. Beyond that, be on guard!

Business gatherings often include discussions where women are continually being greeted, "You really look great today. That dress is outstanding," when all women really crave is attention to the work at hand, and some meaningful advice which they need to accomplish their required tasks.

If you are continually bothered by any man who can influence your career, you owe it to yourself to take corrective action to eliminate the problem—as it will probably only get worse. Simply excuse yourself from his presence and re-enter later in a businesslike manner with a businesslike approach and hope he gets the message. If he doesn't, repeat the action until he does. Bewilder him if necessary. It will cost you nothing. Chances are, he will respect you for it and get down to business. Don't worry, he will still recognize you. Men are built that way.

The actual success of this suggested approach is important to both of you. It will certainly build your self-confidence and esteem and will definitely put him on notice that you are not a "thing," but a bright, strong, tough-minded professional person whose ideals must be recognized first and that you are not playing games.

SYNOPSIS

Men have the power, but women have the purpose. Your purpose will never be achieved if you are not courageously steadfast and unafraid to take a risk. Men will bend to women more easily than women think. Mostly, men want you to prove yourself first and often. Do it. You can! You are strong! You are mentally and physically tougher. You are generally better prepared, better able to keep your cool and have abilities that nurture, reinforce and enhance quality results. Your ultimate goal is to prove to men by demonstrating these powers and by proving that you are quite capable of taking charge. *Never lose sight of the objectives of taking away your share of dominance from males.*

As a woman, you have many advantages and strengths. Find them, build on them and use them to your fullest advantage. I recognize that men have power and control and in some settings you may be lucky to even physically survive, but it won't always be this way. You are a pioneer for those who come later—your kids and my grandkids—and this is a responsibility that generations of women have longed for. I hope parents will soon give their daughters a better advantage by motivating and training them toward their rights, in how to be aggressive and in the need to strive for perfection with success. It's okay for you to play with dolls, learn to cook and so on, but you'd better get up a head of steam when learning how to be challengers and how to react when challenged. On the other hand, I hope parents will instill in their boys the knowledge that girls and women are entitled to as much respect as anyone on earth and should be treated as such.

Meanwhile, you need to take that pioneer spirit and open the path for other women to follow. You need to prove to men that you do indeed measure up, and that you don't have to take their denigrating verbal and physical attacks.

As time advances and more and more women speak out, fewer and fewer men will want to chance the disgrace that results from their demeaning actions. If women "hang in there" and keep the heat on, we may someday soon see men as gentlemen, and women respected.

Never continue in a job you don't enjoy.
If you're happy in what you're doing,
you'll like yourself, you'll have inner peace.
And if you have that, along with physical health,
you will have had more success than you
could possibly have imagined.
—Johnny Carson

15

Politics in a Man's World

To better position yourself in the furtherance of your career, as well as to develop a better understanding of men as you interface with them and follow their lead from day to day, I offer you a summary of the four types of male bosses that you will most probably encounter.

In no matter what field you are working, these men fit a mold and control your destiny, so it is necessary to know and understand them and to learn how to deal with them. It is also important that they get to know you and like you as well. Don't become a man-hater in all of this. You will be tempted to at times, but you can't afford to and still survive. You really need men. I suggest you make good use of their workplace experiences and take advantage of the time you will spend with them. Of course, as you develop your own "woman style," in the end you will be leading them, and they will be seeking you out for help and advice.

Boss Type A

Men are generally a decent lot and I know sometimes you can't understand them. You know the same is said about you. Many men are interested in seeing you advance and are sympathetic to your campaign. Many are young and married to a woman such as yourself, one seeking to achieve a successful career. Many positive thinking, mature, progressive men relate to their new career-seeking women and, believe it or not, they can be on your side.

These are the men with whom to ally yourself or to seek out to become your mentors. They make good bosses because they will back you and make sure you get an even break when the time is right—in a decision meeting or management discussion with promotion, pay raises, individual status or other important career matters as its chief agenda.

Whether you are competing as a peer or interfacing with him in everyday business, be sure to move toward a solid friendship with this man. He may be your next boss or your boss sometime in the future. Build your bridges as you go along. This positive-thinking networking goes with planning your future. You have to visualize that any man or woman you meet, work with, or have any business or workplace dealings with, can be instrumental in your career development and growth. Analyze and be quick to recognize how each one fits into the scheme of things. This approach is important for both men and women because it is good common sense and is evidence of alert thinking.

In my own career, even though I made many mistakes of the tongue, I did muster enough intelligence to treat everyone I trained, mentored or directly supervised with respect and gave them each the necessary attention to help them perform their jobs and maximize their abilities. I never failed to let my boss know when individuals with positive attitudes, resolute enthusiasm and a committed desire to succeed were in my unit. No matter at what level of management, managers are always looking for good people, and increasing numbers of women will be among those considered. It goes with the "surrounding yourself with good people" theory of success.

At any rate, among the many whom I mentored and trained were a senior vice president, three regional vice presidents, a senior merchandising manager and two directors. I've lost count of the number of district managers I trained and mentored. Some even began as hourly employees. I must tell you that it was very rewarding for me to see these people progress, knowing that I had a hand in their success.

As you proceed on the job into management or supervision, always remember that you may be working with or training your next boss or someone who could be your boss as your career unfolds. If you have treated him right and he recognizes your efforts on his behalf, he or she will not forget you. More than likely he or she will find a way to return the positive treatment sometime in the future.

When you are a woman, this camaraderie is even more important because of the necessity of building many strong relationships with men so that when the time comes for the better job or project to be handed out, these men stand up and fight for you. Some will do this and the male boss in Type A is the most likely to give you this help. You need his help badly. Ask for it and use it to your advantage.

So, build as many good, strong relationships with this type of boss as you possibly can. Keep in mind that you must "go along to get along, if you want to succeed. Of course, this relates only to your workplace and working functions. Obviously, other demands by your boss, particularly those of a sexual nature, are out of line, phony, a misuse of your relationship and against the law.

When you get a boss who fits the mold of being interested in you as a person and realizes your strong potential, spend a lot of time learning from him. Build a solid friendship. Let him know that you really appreciate his approach, training and attitude. Help him to like you and all women in general. But don't be phony. That will show through and destroy everything.

Boss Type B

Another group of men is characterized as those who can work with you—but. They are sympathetic to women's issues, but with you they are passive and don't choose to get involved. This is possibly because they don't understand you, your problems or your ideology, and are fearful of being intimidated. This is a gender problem that most men and women have with each other. It won't be solved until both sides take time to understand the other on a more universal basis. Improvements have become evident but they are minuscule.

You can work with boss type B and will make great personal improvement if you work closely with him. Make his goals your goals and he will be quick to respond favorably with a team spirit. Take extra interest in team projects and ask frequent intelligent questions. This way you will learn more from these individuals. Don't be afraid to lightly discuss your personal life with them and they will probably do the same with you. This helps maintain that camaraderie, always makes for a better mold and improves the chemistry between you.

Remember, these men have a great influence in the pecking order and they can be important to your personal progress. Also remember they are human beings with concerns similar to your own and are generally entrusted with large responsibilities.

As you work with these individuals, try to let them see you as an ally, one who they can confide in and rely on when things get tough, especially when their boss becomes overbearing. Become their number one supporter. They will return the favor someday.

Establish when and why bosses in this group are passive and try to avoid you. The clues are easy to spot. It could be that you will be the last one they introduce to another person or to a group gathering. You will be the one left out when the "boys" go to lunch. You will recognize this boss—if you haven't already.

It will take a little work on your part, but you can win them over and it is worth the effort.

One day I met a man who was to manage one of my stores. I was a district manager at the time. It didn't take long to establish that this man was very strong and highly educated with an enormous amount of hands-on experience. Obviously, I treated him with respect, "picked his brain" and, in short order, became one of his close friends, a friendship that lasted for years.

Anyway, I figured that this manager would probably encounter some trouble with one of his four assistant managers, not only because she was experienced and excellent at her job but because she was a strong, self-confident woman. He, being older, was labeled as "old school" and a traditionalist. And he was.

Amazingly enough, in a period of only a few short months, this very bright, strong-willed young woman had won him over and he was not only singing her praises but was shouting to those above about her abilities and potential. It was fortunate timing for this woman, because the company was growing at a faster than normal rate and it was an ideal time for her to establish such a strong working relationship.

She recognized him quickly as a demanding man who gets things done. To make a long story short, that is exactly what she did. She got things done—and fast. He loved it. She made mistakes—he didn't love it and let her know. She corrected her mistakes quickly and let him know—even challenged him to find more mistakes—he loved it. She consistently did good things and made him a partner in her progress.

The other three managers were men. They laid back and watched this woman actually take command of her career by quickly befriending their boss. They learned from both of them that women are as dynamic as men and that above all they shouldn't fear or restrict any woman's growth.

This woman soon went on to become a general manager and later was offered a district manager's position. One of the three men went on to become, and still is today, a regional vice president and, I would like to think partly because of this experience, an ally to women.

When you get a boss who is passive and stand-offish, make it a point to know what his goals are and when he expects to be promoted. Then you can casually make him aware that you are interested in helping him achieve these goals. He will rely on you totally to get the job done and *to be honest with him*. On each assignment, become the "take charge type," so you become the one to whom he delegates the most. If there is a man already established in that spot, diplomatically work your way in, so that you gain a share of attention from the boss. Don't back down or stand aside. You are as good as either of these men. I know, I have seen you work. You know it, too, if you have been paying attention and applying the instructions in this book.

You must always keep in mind that you will have to be more knowledgeable and be better prepared than any man you are competing against. It behooves you, therefore, to stay close to those of experience and knowledge so you can learn from them. Be sure you look for those who practice good judgment and proper use of common sense. These are two valuable abilities lacking in so many working environments today. Good judgment and common sense will help win most of your battles and push you ahead of the crowd.

Boss Type C

Now it gets tougher and you should prepare your emotions for a test and a workout. Here is the group of bosses who at times are considered to be S.O.B.s by the men they control. With women, they are always S.O.B.s, unfriendly, antagonistic, chauvinistic, mostly sexists who would rather not have you around. Your presence ruins their day, confuses their thinking, and makes them use an improved, more respectful vocabulary, and they hate that. They really are forced to clean up their act.

They will ignore you or let you go unnoticed but will pigeonhole you in a job slot or keep you seated in the back of the room every chance they get. They either don't like you or are fearful of your abilities and potential. It may not show, but you scare them. These men are very difficult to deal with and unfortunately can be found in greater numbers than you would like to see. You will rarely, if ever, be given credit for good achievements. They will probably treat your outstanding achievements as the work of someone else or ignore them altogether. They will ridicule you at review time and will be miserly when pay increases or bonuses are handed out. They look for you to make mistakes. If you are married, they hope you get pregnant and will not only be happy to see you on leave to have the baby, but will do everything they can to see that you don't come back. In general, they are not good candidates for fairness and understanding. They will make you cry and put you into a world of emotional upset.

This type will never change in your lifetime. They are chauvinists to the core. This is a heavy accusation but, I assure you, it is accurate.

When working for these men, your standards and work quality must be better than anyone else's. You have to learn strong self-motivation, maintain a high professional profile and a low-key woman image. You must always carry a traditional label with these bosses. You must be businesslike at all times and still keep up your performance. The higher your motivation and positive profile, the better chances you have of survival. You just have to "hang in there." This is a tough assignment because you are not being motivated by your boss or the environment.

Don't be victimized by setbacks or a manipulative experience created by a discriminatory type C boss. A positive male mentor (like boss type A) might be great for your career and training, but if he is followed by a self-centered, insensitive, dictator whose main objective is to put you out the door, out of his sight, simply because you are a woman, then you must not only prepare yourself for that potential setback, but you must convince yourself that it will not destroy your will or your commitment.

Men and women get fired from jobs. That's a reality and many times unavoidable. But getting fired is not always a bad thing. Most of the time a new job is the best thing that can happen and proves more enjoyable and sometimes better paying and more in line with your chemistry and career goals.

I recently had a client who was victimized as described. Bobbi had a strong mentor who was devoted to her training and success. She had strong desire and a total commitment to achievement as well, Unfortunately, her type A boss left the company. She moved around somewhat within the company, got promoted, but one day she was assigned a type C boss. From day one she received no training or guidance of any kind; his frequent inspections came on her assigned day off, forcing her to change her schedule; and the review of her work was purposefully, continually negative and obviously intended to destroy her and make her quit.

She was eventually assigned a particular task that was predetermined to result in her failure. It placed her in a life-threatening position and in an environment requiring special police training, which was not provided for her. It was impossible for her to carry out this assignment in good conscience. She was fired for her inability to follow instructions, carry out assignments and poor work history. In earlier assignments this same woman received continual "very good" performance appraisals, pay increases and even a promotion.

You want to get away from this type of boss as quickly as possible. It won't be accomplished in a day, week or month. However, you must work every angle to achieve this. You will begin to see why it is important to lay the early groundwork for your career by befriending as many people as you can. With this type of boss, you can use help—maybe someone you helped or befriended will come through for you.

There are really only two things you can do to help yourself when you have boss type C:

1. Work like hell to get him promoted.

2. Move to another area or even change jobs. Do this *as soon as you know* you are stuck and going nowhere. Don't put it off.

These bosses are not good for your career and are the ones who refuse to develop, mentor or promote women. They will offer you much but deliver nothing.

Boss Type D

Finally, there is a small group of misfits you might encounter. These are the ones who live in yesteryear and can be described as the "disconsolate maniacs" who absolutely abhor the thought of talking to, working with or training any woman at any time. They just won't do it—even if their jobs depend on it. And if it comes to that, they rely on the typical lousy judgment of the "good ol' boys" network to salvage their jobs.

This group I have personally observed in action many times in my 44 years in business. I never liked them or enjoyed their company. Among a great many other things, they are boring.

The only direction you can be given for dealing with this group is to avoid them, erstwhile you will lose all of your hard-earned self-stuff and end up a "basket case," blaming yourself because you are a woman. If it is any consolation, this group of renegades is also a severe problem to aspiring men. Someday you will not have to contend with them because their style of management and supervision will self-destruct and yours will replace it.

Again, keep in mind that as I offer this direction and guidance, I give you over four decades of managing experience in applications mostly with women. You may choose to question or challenge a portion or all of my descriptions of these groups. You won't, of course, if you have experience already. If you are inclined to question what is offered here, then you are in for a very bad time with those bosses who are types C and D and will not benefit much from those who are types A and B. I urge you to restudy this and identify who your boss really is and remember the story of Red Riding Hood.

The last two groups are the ones responsible for the stagnation of women in middle management and the establishment of the "glass ceiling" concept. It may be an emotional strain on you to walk away from these types but you have no choice if you truly want to achieve your career goals. Don't dilly-dally in this predicament, for it is definitely a downer and a dead-end for your career. Don't be like so many other women in the past who just "put up" with this crowd far too long and as a result destroyed their initiative, motivation and eventually their self-confidence. You will never "learn to know what good is" in this atmosphere—they just won't let you.

If men were treated this way, they would have "packed it in" for new sights and sounds long ago. They just get tough-minded with themselves and do it. You will have to get tough with yourself also. Shed some tears if you want, but just don't accept these conditions.

Most women who have excelled and reached the senior circuit have made these tough decisions, generally at a time when they had peaked in performance. They realized the necessity for change and made the move. They obviously learned the "if it is to be—it is up to me" theory and followed that lead. You must do the same.

Don't treat this chapter lightly. Keep these thoughts uppermost in your mind. If you constantly use this book as a guide, you will have a better chance of success. After all, your success is the primary goal of this book.

One more point, if and when things get bad at work and depression sets in, pick up this book and reread the motivating and uplifting passages that will put you back on track and make you feel special and good again.

SYNOPSIS

Ally yourself with Type A bosses—seek them out as mentors, true friends and reliable influences. Protect them and they will protect you. They are very good for your career.

Work as closely as possible in a businesslike manner with type B. They are on your side but are passive. Capture as much experienced knowledge as you can and let them know you are in their camp and are reliable.

With type C you will have to play "hard ball." They don't know any other way. Work hard and use very high standards Don't challenge them unless you can prove a better way. Work with them as long as you can, then take steps to move away—for your career's sake.

Type D—avoid them—get away from them as quickly as possible. They will destroy your will and all of the "self things" dear to you.

Risk! Risk anything! Care no more
for the opinion of others, for those voices.
Do the hardest thing on earth for you.
Act for yourself. Face the truth.
—Katherine Mansfield

16

Take the Risk— You Have to Do What You Have to Do

One of the greatest adventures of living is taking charge of your life. It is adventurous because there is no road map to detail how you should do it. (And don't expect me in this chapter or book to outline a program for you either—it just can't happen.) Women of any class, group, age or financial status need to give this matter their fullest attention, especially since women are more involved with who they are, what they are, where they want to go and how they want to get there. Now is the time to lay claim to the new advantages you can enjoy in the workplace. You are on the threshold of moving into workplaces and prestige positions that heretofore were privately held by men—and you can do it in large numbers. But each of you has to take charge of your life and organize your thoughts, spelling out what you really want. It has to be a plan, a lifelong plan, that focuses on your true desires and aspirations, a real plan wherein you can actually visualize yourself attaining the enjoyable things in life that you really want and deserve and can now have and enjoy. Someone should arrange a major celebration for this because it is a major breakthrough for women. It is like winning the cold war.

When you analyze it, that is really what this book is about, winning. I have delivered a message to you that thus far has conditioned you for your new world of opportunities—opportunities your mother and grandmother could only dream about, but were reserved and marked for men only.

These new advantages are real for you. You can have them. You can really overcome adversity and have the good life. First, you will have to take the needed steps to put it together and you must also be ready to take the *risks*.

If I have successfully done my job and awakened your thoughts and tempted your desires to really attain these precious goals, then the next step to discuss is your reception to taking a risk. Successful risk-taking involves aggressively attacking your goals.

The risks I want to emphasize are the gutsy ones you will need to take to get attention and get ahead in your job, the ones you must accept head on if you really want to reach those worthwhile heights in your career. Some of these can be demanding and challenging to your mind and will. Some are so wild they will strain your conservative nature and overload your stress capacity. As you get pressured in a specific situation, you will realize that the only way to reach new heights or to improve your career is to take that risk. You must take it! You can't turn back! You have to put yourself in a position of total commitment and you may have to put everything you are, including your reputation, on the line. Some risky adventures are that heavy. For example, think of the risks that astronauts must take, especially after witnessing that fatal disaster on January 28, 1986.

Women have often been accused of being too timid to take chances. In some men's circles this accusation stands even today. However, more and more women like you are standing up to the most challenging uncertainties and are enjoying the rewards of success. Self-determination is what risk is all about. Those who have it know within themselves they can take the risk, because they have determined to bring their lives in line with their dreams. Many women have gathered enough courage and perseverance to take on serious risks. If the reward of success is worth it, then the risk is worth it.

On the other hand, the vast majority of women still fear taking even the smallest risks and often find various excuses to avoid them. These women, for one reason or another, still lack the self-confidence and commitment to seize the new advantages women can achieve, and they continue to look for excuses as to why they can't have them. They are great examples of the cliche, "If you don't want to do something, any excuse will do." Once again, you really have to want something, you really have to make a commitment to achieve your dreams. You have to think, "Me first."

Today your wildest career dreams are within your grasp and if you really, truly want to be part of that small percentage of people who achieve and enjoy the good life, you now have that chance.

Risking all cannot be better said than by authors Jean Ray Laury, Terri P. Tepper, and Nona Dawe Tepper, when addressing the feminist issue in *The New Entrepreneurs*. They say,

> Risk everything all of the time and quit trying to be safe. Once you're willing to risk your whole reputation on something, then you can leap forward. That's when you really have the possibility of moving out from whatever you've done before. We spend an awful lot of time defending ourselves and protecting ourselves and being safe and comfortable. If we're expecting to move ahead we have to take chances and we have to take risks and we have to do things that might make

us look foolish if they don't work out, and that's okay. It's okay to be wrong. It's okay to fail if you try something and though in a sense it failed, you're still a winner. You still come out ahead. I don't see how there is any way if you risk things, you can really lose. There is so much that you learn; there is so much of value in what you create.

The only advantage risk has over you is your fear. Risks and fear are the excitement of life. They make life more interesting and dispel boredom. Fear of taking a risk can turn a hero into a coward, can turn the opportunity of wealth into a financial desperation. Fear of actually living the life you deserve will drive you to a secluded mind and spirit and destroy your desired accomplishments.

When in doubt, shun the fear, take the risk and you will be a much happier person for it.

In my career, as in anyone's who takes on responsibility and decision-making, I have put my job on the line a number of times, either to help someone or to make a point I felt very strongly about. You can't be involved as decision-maker unless you have the guts and take the risks required for success. Nor can you jump over tall buildings without realizing and accepting the possibility that you might fall.

It may be that the race is not always to the swift,
nor the battle to the strong—but
that's the way to bet.
—Damon Runyon

There is risk in everything you do—when making big decisions on the job, in planning your personal life (marriage, having a baby) and your career. You must stretch yourself to meet the requirements. You can't win the lottery unless you buy a ticket. You can't become Number One without putting yourself in jeopardy. You can't do anything really big in life without facing some risk. Don't be intimidated by it.

To be the person you want to be, to be successful, happy and at peace with yourself, "YOU GOTTA DO WHAT YOU GOTTA DO."

However, always keep these Murphy's laws in mind, as they will apply at different points along the process of your career:

Law #1 says: Nothing is as easy as it looks.
Law #2 says: Everything takes longer than you think.
Law #5 says: If anything just cannot go wrong, it will anyway.
Law #8 says: If everything seems to be going well, you have obviously overlooked something.

And the one that you really have to be ready for is Murphy's law of thermodynamics, which says: Things get worse under pressure.

Murphy's laws are perfect at explaining stress in a way that brings you down to earth and helps balance your emotions and thinking. It is amazing that these laws are so on target with life. More important, they take the seriousness of the pitfalls, make them human and ease the pain of the adversity. I am glad they came along. I have laughed with them throughout my career.

Challenging Risk Head-On

Men address risk a great deal differently from you. This is one aspect of their general character that is worthwhile and you must learn it.

While some women have stood up to the challenge and taken some healthy risks, men still stereotype women as weak-kneed and quick to accept easier, safer alternatives. Naturally, it is easier and safer and maybe less hurtful, but it also is a "woman thing" in their eyes. Most men still see you as a dependent, delicate soul, unable to carry anything, fix anything or do anything too strenuous or mind-boggling.

Similarly, they see you as the woman who went into a tizzy when her son announced his plans to play football, when he wanted to drive the car (alone) on his sixteenth birthday, or when duty called and he had to go into the service. In all of these instances most women cave in to despair. They dwell on the risks and place themselves into emotional disarray. Obviously, some of the things are "iffy," but none are so serious as to warrant a strong negative reaction.

How do you overcome this attitude? First, it will help if you do not at first think of the adverse possibilities, but rather think of the joy and fun these activities will afford your child. Make a personal commitment that you will not overreact and will accept the outcome.

This would be the same approach to use when you are confronted with risks of your own. Don't dwell on the negative. Emphasize the positive aspects and benefits. Apply the same approach to workplace issues and assignments and the man in charge will find favor with you and will not question your attitude or abilities with regard to the tasks he assigns you. He knows that the job has to get done and until he sees you accepting risks and hears from your lips that you are not afraid and are capable of handling risks, he will always take the alternate route and avoid you.

Let's change that image.

The American College Dictionary defines risk as—"exposure to the chance of injury or loss; a hazard or dangerous chance of loss." That describes it well, although it may sound severe. You can always lighten the burden of risk by knowing more about the subject or project than anyone else. By stacking the deck with learned knowledge, you can take the obviously heavy burden, as others view it, dilute it and direct the results in your favor. Do your homework and it will really lighten the burden in your favor.

Case in point: A general manager I knew was constantly having replenishment problems in a sizeable area of his large store. For some reason, buyers and merchandising people had had a long-standing breakdown in communication with each other, which left the general manager in a very unhealthy customer relations quandary. It got to a point where he hated to go to work because of the customer abuse he received and the terrible employee morale.

Letter after letter went forward to those responsible, to the merchandising manager and, finally, to the vice president of merchandising. By now the general manager was stretched about as far out with frustration as he could go. He had already risked his standing with the buyer by going over the buyer's head and contacting the merchandising manager, and he was likewise in deep trouble with the merchandising manager because he had gone over his head also. What to do? Take one more risk! He decided to make the president of the company a partner to his problem. Now, this is a real no-no, the mortal sin of all mortal sins in almost any business circle. In a brief but precise, factual way, he wrote this risky letter to the president. He committed that political mortal sin—one that could cause phones to ring with more threatening verbiage than I would write here.

Within a week, an answer came back. The president, the vice president, the merchandising manager and the buyer made an unannounced visit to his store. The president wasn't interested in catching the general manager or store people off guard, but rather in attending to the problem first hand, because it was a problem so long neglected and one that might well exist in many other units.

Doing Your Homework

During the review of the out-of-stock condition, the president asked the general manager what he had done about such atrocious conditions. The general manager, a capable individual who was well-schooled in the problem and potential outcome, advised the chief executive that he had written a seemingly endless number of letters, had sent pictures and had made numerous phone calls to all the necessary people. The president asked him if he had copies of the letters, times, dates of the phone calls and so on.

In anticipation of all of this, the savvy general manager had already requested the correspondence file and was immediately able to produce the mounds of correspondence, dates and times. Now in this type of circumstance there are winners and losers. Needless to say, this general manager won.

The general manager's stock-in-trade skyrocketed, not only for his clever ability to document and produce evidence, but even more for putting his job on the line and really sticking his neck out to prove a point and carry out his responsibilities to his customers.

He took a gigantic risk. He put his job and career on the line, but because he had been so hands-on to the problem, he was thoroughly aware of the entire fiasco. He knew exactly who and what caused it to happen and covered himself thoroughly with well-documented communication. He won and was gratefully rewarded with good words. He did his homework well, while others resorted to rhetoric for their salvation.

The lesson here is how to lighten the burden of risk-taking—that is, you must document and keep records of anything that could cause you pain or hurt you in your career. A daily diary or log of important events, calls and so on, will always pay off when the going gets tough and you find yourself in a challenged position. You, as a woman, must always document any negative personal remarks or challenges, harassing innuendos or sexual advances for future reference. This is a must! Proof and facts will help your cause and put you in a strong position. Having them will generally satisfy anyone with power, but you must have proof and facts—hard copies of written documentation—if you find yourself in litigation or in front of the E.E.O.C., or you do not have a case.

Always Protect Yourself

In this scenario, the buying division did not have taking care of business as a priority. Not attending to business for weeks on end was real evidence of poor management and poor communication. You will probably be subjected to similar problems in your career.

Here is another gimmick I used that was a savior. When you are repeatedly communicating in a problem situation and are not getting an answer, not getting the problem solved and just feeling totally ignored, write one more letter to the neglectful individual (even if the person is in-house) and summarize in detail everything—times you wrote, times you called about the problem and so on, but give the individual one final chance to respond and correct the situation. Send a copy to his boss. Then make an extra copy, in addition to the one in your file, mail it to yourself at home and keep it safely stored away for future use. Don't open it. Invariably, a person so incapable or too lazy to address a problem or simply to answer a question will resort to many antics to cover himself before his boss, not the least of which will be to describe you, a woman, to his boss in the normal stereotypical way, while trying to lie his way out of the situation. "I never received any correspondence," he says. But, by producing a carbon copy in a sealed envelope, "franked" with the date and time you sent it—well, it's hard for anyone not to take your side. You have real evidence, proof and facts. It did require some extra work, but the risk was eased substantially by keeping good records and using them advantageously. Even if his boss goes against you because you are a woman, your sealed envelope becomes more precious as you ascend the ladder for support.

SPECIAL NOTE: Never drop a surprise problem letter on the desk of a senior executive or the president of a company without giving all of those along the way a chance to correct their problems. However, if all fail to respond, even after a few follow-ups, then you should go to the higher authority. That's another risk. It is also one that I have seen some women take when dealing with the "good ol' boys" group. It is one that will get results—and in your favor if you are documented thoroughly. It's extra work—but it pays off. It worked for me. It will work for you, too.

SYNOPSIS

In summary, I guess you could say that life is one big risk, but it doesn't have to be something to shy away from. Please don't go through life missing a good time because you are afraid to drive a freeway. Don't stay at home at night because you are afraid of the dark. Don't miss the adventure of a chanced winning in a confrontation that could have career benefits. Think and plan your way through it, then go for it. But don't do anything stupid either. Let common sense rule. If you get into a risk situation, remember to have a thorough knowledge of all particulars, including those of the opposite side. Always document important matters and have the pertinent ones ready for evidence. In confrontations, you deal in facts, especially when things get heavy and someone's career may be on the line. Always protect yourself with written communications.

As the *New Entrepreneur* said, "If we're expecting to move ahead, we have to take risks and we have to do things that might make us look foolish if they don't work out, and that's okay." You have to do what you have to do.

Never make an apology until you are accused.
—King Edward I

When they say, 'It's a jungle out there,'
we all shout, 'Amen!' The difference is,
in a jungle you use brute force,
in the workplace, intelligent common sense.
—Jack McAllen

17

The Professional List of Positive Points that Promise Help— The 4-P List

For your convenience and ready reference, I have developed a list of 66 *professional positive points* that *promise* to help you along the way. I recommend you keep them handy and reread them frequently. Some may be repetitions of instructions from previous chapters, and some you may already know; all are important. This professional list of positive points that promise help is not presented in an order of importance, nor is one superior to the rest.

Use this 4-P List when you begin a career or are already knee-deep in some form of career activity and need some reinforcement. Having been there, I realize that days run together and move by quickly, every day tasks demand your fullest attention and the boss always has special projects that his boss has demanded to be done *now!* Even your own personal plans and special projects suffer the hectic pace that greets every day, not to mention the double compression of keeping balance in your home life and its demands.

When they say, "It's a jungle out there," we all shout, "Amen!" The difference is, in a jungle you have to use brute force, whereas, in the workplace you need intelligent, common sense. A good attitude and understandable communication are key. That is why the positive points are not an attempt to tell you how to live your life or to suggest stupidity, rather they are offered just to nudge you back on track when you wander off the true path that will make you a quality feminine leader, an example for other women and the pacesetter for future aspiring novices.

Most women agree they should not pick up men's habits and try to adjust to their world. Don't we have too many "good ol' boys" now? Rather, women are at their best using their skills as they carry out their own agenda for proper inclusion into this newly-begotten, uncharted working atmosphere. Your advantage is your power and ability to pick and choose. On the other hand, some things men do are good and you would be foolish not to copy them. Many things, however, are stained and strained from traditional overuse and need changing. Examples of these are repeatedly represented in this book.

Each of these "Positive Points" are from actual experiences, not textbook theory. Each has its own basis in fact and has either been witnessed by me, or I was the originator of the thought. Nonetheless, they are all important. They do not appear in any particular order of importance nor is one superior to the other. Watch out! The men around may steal them.

1. Learn to communicate in a positive, professional way. Use good grammar, sentence structure and spelling. Can't do this now? Learn. It tells everyone who and what you are.

2. Listen to your staff when they speak, offer ideas or seek your help.
3. Follow up on the things you said you would do for them—never leave them stranded and never keep them from performing their tasks.
4. Learn and practice assertive communication—stating your wishes, instructions and feelings directly and with complete honesty.
5. Learn and practice the real art of give-and-take. Libraries are full of this stuff for in-depth study.
6. When alone in the company of men, try to control the conversation to prevent your being left out. For starters, you will at least need to have a surface knowledge of sports, politics, current events and government.
7. Learn to become tough-minded to prevent getting a wishy-washy, wimpy reputation and to be able to establish a work-from-strength capability. Always work from strength.
8. Learn to protect yourself from in-fighting and criticism by becoming an authority in your own job function and by learning the jobs of those around you, including the responsibilities of your boss.
9. Every morning tell yourself how great you are and how much stronger and smarter you are than your peers. I know you are; you have convinced me.
10. Set achievable goals so you will know the feeling of success, and prevent frustration from out-of-sight requirements that are impossible to achieve.
11. Be positive about everything, especially yourself, your attitude and how you see life.
12. If you possess physical beauty, enjoy it, but don't build anything on it, for one day it will fade. If you are not beautiful physically—you have one less thing to worry about.
13. Always try to be "up" and ready for the action. Your associates will like it and so will your boss.

14. Become an overachiever so you will be on a par, at least, with the few very aggressive men and far ahead of the majority.
15. Always project a feminine appearance and attitude and preserve it. It is a very strong asset—one thing he really can't copy.
16. Become aggressive in your work and, when it pays off, demand recognition. Do it in a charming, tough-minded way.
17. Maintain and utilize your nurturing and supportive attitude. This also is an asset and something men need but don't have. Don't overreact to a sudden display of emotion.
18. Learn to control your emotions and never let men see you cry. Men see it as a weakness.
19. Use positive reinforcement frequently and really mean it from the heart. A phony compliment is cheap and a turn off.
20. Be indispensable by making yourself more valuable than anyone you work with, including your boss. If things get bad, you will still have a job.
21. Make sure you know what job performance errors you are making. Seek out your performance appraisal for evaluation.
22. Always display a relaxed confidence and keep your cool when crisis decisions must be made.
23. Treat associates with respect and praise them when they show good results.
24. Do learn to become results-oriented—your boss is.
25. Develop and practice a good problem-solving method so you can give good guidance and control unfriendly situations.
26. Instill a family-friendly attitude in your subordinates and train them to behave in that spirit.

27. Be enthusiastic about all you do. Shout it out so those around you will capture and follow the lead. Enthusiasm is said to move like a wildfire.
28. Get ahead of your competition and stay ahead by seeking further education through college classes, seminars and so on.
29. Always be ready to make a full commitment—*always.*
30. Do become a gambler, a risk-taker. Life is more exciting and you become more involved.
31. Always keep an "ace in the hole." Don't play all of your cards at one time—ever.
32. Always find the good in a bad situation and always find the good in weak people.
33. Never arrive late for anything important, especially the boss's meetings.
34. Put men at ease by being honest and letting them know where you stand.
35. Practice developing a fascinating vocabulary. A strong vocabulary is always a confidence builder.
36. Use men's fear of women in the workplace to your advantage, but never make them look foolish.
37. Plan to be at least as good as your best competitor—you will need to be better to beat him.
38. Do persevere, persevere, persevere.
39. Do it right the first time. You don't have time to keep doing it over.
40. Inaugurate and promote a good networking system with women equal in status and above.
41. Always protect your staff and always be there when they need you.
42. Give your people the authority that goes with their job; let them make choices and decisions freely. Insist on it—don't let them off the hook.
43. Select and keep only the best team players on your staff.
44. Become the dominant player on your boss's team.

45. Find your peak achieving time of the day, and work on your most important tasks then.
46. Seek out the stumbling blocks in your daily work and career and eliminate them one at a time—but work on them.
47. Set priorities daily and attack the most important one first. It's probably the top priority on your boss's list. Use a "do" sheet.
48. Mentally evaluate your work life and be ready for tough decisions—with alternatives.
49. Remember that luck comes to you when you are working the hardest.
50. Look at your job as a challenge, not as a drag.
51. Avoid stress by developing a healthy approach to your job. Exercise and good eating habits are essential.
52. Accept recognition graciously and appreciate it as something to be savored and flaunted.
53. Accept all promotions—each one leads to the next and one will be your ultimate goal.
54. Always, always set a good example.
55. Tie your career goals to your personal life goals so they will not conflict with each other.
56. Practice being clever, unique and unusual—but don't overdo it.
57. Work for a company that is progressive and growing. It is much easier on you and hastens personal growth.
58. Practice learning how to win; be able to identify the feeling, then never accept any other, but don't compromise all for victory.
59. Know what the rewards of your efforts will be. If you don't know, get a quick answer.
60. Try to make things better in the workplace, even if they are okay.
61. Always tell a disgruntled or unhappy employee that you are trying to help him when relations are strained.

62. Learn when to stand pat on an issue, learn when to give in to a more intelligent approach, and learn when to back off from a bad situation.
63. Develop unquestionable integrity, for this is your best advantage when you are being personally challenged.
64. Build a good relationship with your boss, with his peers and with his boss so you have a good playing field. Spotlight yourself as often as you can.
65. Remember, if *he* can do it, you can do it.
66. Be a professional—always.

God knows, if you do all of the things recommended in this list, you will no doubt someday be seated to His right. If you miss a few, He won't be surprised. If you miss too many, you will be the loser. One thing is certain, men don't subscribe to all of these positive principles. I don't know how God feels about that, but I do know that the more you use them, the further ahead you will be.

My reference to God is for purposes of levity only. And, even though it is a light-hearted treatment, I do not intend to diminish the importance of your response to the 4-P list.

Some of these are my own positive approaches that have been developed from hard-earned experiences. Others are directions I have learned from others or have read—and adopted. Still others have stood the test of time and are still pertinent. They are a compilation of worthwhile, useful guidance tools that will make you stronger, more successful, a real quality individual, happy and a winner.

Many points on the list are very aggressive, a quality really lacking in the workplace today. Too many workers are still looking for the easiest buck or some "cake" job. Others have improved (for example, in the car industry). Still another group thinks the world owes them. While we are doing a better job of making cars, I am sorry to say we are doing a lousy job of selling them.

Many successful car salesmen work and use good selling techniques and are devoted to their craft. On the other hand, far too many others are complacent, use poor selling techniques, are lazy and constantly complain about their lack of success and take-home pay. There are few women in this industry. It is one ripe for infiltration and can be easy pickings if you learn the trade and work hard.

I don't mean to single out only car salesmen as those most guilty of poor work habits. I use them merely as a classic example of an industry that really hasn't promoted women in its ranks (except in manufacturing) and as an industry that is vulnerable to the aggressive woman. I see a woman car salesperson as a natural and very successful addition to this industry's showrooms.

Opportunities exist for women to excel in every work emphasis. Just don't become complacent; seek out those opportunities and strive to be the best.

In every male-dominated workplace, far too many men sit on their duffs, milking their jobs for all they're worth. An aggressive woman entering this workplace could quickly take over their empire and begin to run it properly. No, it won't be easy and you will take many "hits," but after you survive, you will reap the rewards. And these rewards will be worth the effort in many ways.

All you have to do is show better results. You really can do it. And the time is ripe, now.

This 4-P list and this book will help get you there. The rest has to come from your desire and commitment. I am sincerely convinced you can achieve all of this.

Remember not only to say the right thing
in the right place, but far more difficult still,
to leave unsaid the wrong thing
at the tempting moment.
—Benjamin Franklin

18

A List of Disciplined Directions Designed To Prevent Disaster— The 4-D List

Since no one is perfect and most of us surrender to some form of laziness, this lengthy list that outlines a disciplined approach to preventing career disasters may prove to be a real challenge for you. You will have to reach down into yourself for more self-discipline if you are to receive the full benefits from these directions. They do serve as another all-important tool and guide to help mold your future into a successful, happy one and to help prevent disaster.

Many of the weaknesses outlined in the following list result from poor habits or weak or insufficient training, or they may be a part of your traditional upbringing. Whatever the source, they must be corrected and the key to doing this is, once again, *self-discipline.* As you pursue working and correcting the disciplined directives, you will automatically feel like a stronger person. This will improve your overall image dramatically.

As you begin applying these instructions and directions, most specifically the items in the 4-P and the 4-D Lists, you will feel a definite change in yourself. Your self-confidence and enthusiasm will build. All of your "self things" will take a leap forward, making you feel strong and sure. The more of these you incorporate into your work ethic and philosophy, the greater your strength and self-worth.

Assuredly, as you progress, those around you will quickly notice the change. Most will applaud you and feel more comfortable and secure being around you. Nobody likes to cheer for a loser; nobody likes to work for one either. Strong employees migrate toward a good boss. They likewise move away from one who is weak and who doesn't serve their needs. Weak bosses cause employees to look to each other for answers and support. Employees then become dominant and begin to make their own rules or try to take over altogether. Surprisingly enough, they really don't want to take the lead—all they want to do is their job. They know they don't get paid for running the show, but good employees know somebody has to lead.

You can guard against all of these pitfalls in your entrepreneurship by following the guidelines in this book. I suggest you refer to this book and reread it often. Keep it as a handy reference.

The list of "Disciplined Directions Designed to Prevent Disaster" (the 4-D List) is not presented in any order of importance, nor is any one point superior to another. Each point is very important.

1. Don't take the criticism of poor work you did or were responsible for as a personal affront. Seldom, if ever, is it intended that way. Just correct it.

2. Never challenge your boss or any superior when he/she corrects your work, and never resort to making excuses. They are only trying to help you improve. Give them a break, just take note and tell them you will correct it.
3. Never go into an emotional frenzy or break down in tears when being reprimanded. If you're wrong, admit it and promise to correct it.
4. Don't hold bitterness or disgruntled feelings inside only to blow it all someday with an outburst. Discuss things with the boss as they happen.
5. Don't go to bed at night harboring bad feelings that should have been corrected during the day.
6. Refrain from discussing "women things" when trying to infiltrate a male-dominated conversation (*i.e.,* P.M.S., husband's job success, credit cards, babysitters, maternity leave, kids and other stereotypical topics).
7. Don't avoid conversation with the "good ol' boys" simply because you know they are skeptical of you and uncomfortable with your conversation. Let them know you can converse on just about any topic.
8. Don't be afraid to go head-to-head with your boss when you feel strongly about your position. Most bosses like good verbal contact and, anyway, they hate to lose good help.
9. Don't feel or portray an insecure image.
10. If you play where you work—*it will ruin you.* There are plenty of players outside your workplace. Protect your reputation.
11. The only one who wins in an argument is the one who walks away. Avoid arguments.
12. Don't go out of your way to destroy or damage the ego of a man you work with.
13. Don't ever learn to lose or it will become a habit.
14. Don't accept mediocrity or poor performance from anyone on your team.

15. Once you achieve success—move quickly on to the next challenge. Don't become complacent.
16. Don't let success overwhelm you or make you uncomfortable.
17. If you procrastinate—he won't.
18. If you vacillate between being a career woman or a domestic engineer—one will serve you, the other could put you in servitude.
19. Don't avoid taking risks out of weakness.
20. If you look for the easy way out, you can easily find it and the stereotypical remarks that go with it.
21. You just can't avoid college or higher education. He doesn't. It is the basic ingredient.
22. Don't put yourself down—ever. Others will pick up on it and help you beat yourself.
23. Don't understate or underrate your abilities. If you know you are good—show it.
24. Keep self-doubt and self-criticism to yourself—and get rid of it.
25. Don't ever let men hear you verbally destroy yourself.
26. Don't ever complain down in rank—always complain up—to the boss. He/She is the only one who can correct the problem.
27. Don't be afraid to think that you are good.
28. If you don't want to do something, any excuse will do, so avoid excuses and don't accept them from those who report to you.
29. If you stand around waiting for things to happen to you, they won't—make them happen.
30. Don't linger in a dead-end job—move on.
31. Don't be afraid to quit your job for a better position in another company, and don't put it off.
32. Never, but never, quit your job until you have another to go to.
33. Don't take your eyes off your goal (target)—keep it in front of you wherever you are.

34. Don't criticize company policy in front of peers or subordinates. Policies and procedures are there for a purpose.
35. The purpose of your company is to make a profit. Be profit-oriented.
36. If you must complain about anything, always have a workable solution ready to offer.
37. Remember—you get paid only for results. Anything else may be a decoy.
38. Don't work in the wrong area on the wrong project—your effort will go unnoticed and wasted. Find out what the boss is working on and get into the action.
39. Don't job-hop. Too many jobs converts your resume into a laundry list.
40. Don't leave your staff in the dark about your wants and goals. Let them know where you are going.
41. Don't gossip about your boss if you can't say anything nice. Be loyal to him/her.
42. Don't carry loyalty to your company too far. You are selling your labor for salary. Don't confuse this with anything else. Company loyalty to you will never be greater than your loyalty to the company.
43. Don't put all men into one category. They are not all bad.
44. Never say the following:

    "We've always done it this way."
    "It won't work."
    "That's a man's job."
    "You can get away with it; you're a man."

45. You can never be successful on your own if you don't like and can't manage people, or if you have a hangup about men.
46. Don't become a casualty by participating in loose company talk or office politics. Learn who the active participants are and stay away from them, for eventually they will fall and take you down with them.
47. Don't expect praise and never ask for it. No news is good news.

48. "Don't tell people your problems—20% don't care; 80% are glad you've got them."—Lou Holtz, coach at Notre Dame University.
49. If you spend too much time watching television news or reading the front page of the newspaper, remember all of it is overkill and will plunge you into a world of despair and self-blame.
50. New opportunity won't come by express mail. It just pops in—normally on Monday, but sometimes on Friday.
51. Don't ever forget who you are and what you stand for.
52. Eliminate people on your staff who are not doing the job. Remember they are either with you or against you. Be tough-minded.
53. Don't treat pregnancy leave as a vacation—keep in touch; have work sent home to you, etc.
54. Don't listen to rumors.
55. Keep out of the way of your staff. Let them do their jobs and hold them to their responsibilities. Don't resort to the philosophy that, "If you want something done right, you must do it yourself." That is a sign of poor teaching and poor managing. You can't do everything yourself.
56. Don't become your own worst enemy by being too hard on yourself. Give the job your best shot, then rejoice in it. When you fail, pick yourself back up quickly.
57. Don't forget to smell the roses.
58. Don't accept the fact that you are *just* common, but do always use common sense.
59. Don't just take what they give you; take what you want.
60. Keep these lists and this book dear to your heart.
61. Remember who wrote it—he really cares about you.

Common Sense Tips for Women

Here are some further common sense tips for you as a woman:

- Learn how to express yourself effectively. People are not mind readers. Make certain they fully understand what you say, but make sure you say it.
- If you want something out of life, ask for it and don't be afraid. The most that can be said to you is—NO!
- In a man's working world, you won't get as much time to prepare or practice as a man would, so work quickly and try to anticipate coming events by keeping abreast of company activities. Acquaint yourself with somebody who has an accurate pipeline, someone you can trust for good advance information.
- Always use a calm approach to everything and never get into a loud or heavy vocal confrontation.
- Oppose anything you don't agree with, but acknowledge the other person's point of view—stand your ground when you know you are right.
- Never apologize for anything that you did if you have given the incident sufficient prior consideration.
- Light sexual situations are normal between men and women; don't overstate sexual harassment or cry wolf too often. If you don't know how to control these situations—learn. You must learn in order to manage and lead men. This may also apply in other life encounters.
- Protect your reputation. It goes with you from job to job and company to company. Your reputation with your clients, customers or others who rely on your services, likewise, goes with you. You are important to them; they rely on your honesty, good judgment and good reputation.
- It is still acceptable and nice if men open doors for you, pay the tab and help you with heavy objects. Accept it with their compliments. It is still their way of communicating without hitting on you. Anyway, it's merely a payback for the many nice things you will do for them.
- How you handle sexual harassment is very important. You can either make enemies or friends. Remember, men are still in the "unlearning stage" of trying to adjust to this new

phenomenon. Good taste is one of your better qualities. Practice and use it freely in these situations. Let others get the bad rap for overreacting to the sexual stuff. I don't suggest that you accept it, by any means, but be prudent in any event.

- Just because men by habit use unprofessional, sometimes abrasive, other times degrading language, doesn't mean (1) that you should accept it or (2) you should copy it and use it. You are not a man and, if overheard by senior executives using such language, it can cost you a good reputation—stay feminine and be of higher quality. It is amazing how effective a strong, polished vocabulary can be.

You obviously bought this book for a reason and most probably so that you can improve or increase your potential and maybe even take advantage of the better opportunities women have today. Whatever the reason, please use it and be guided by it. Don't just put it on the shelf and procrastinate away the advantages it can give you.

SYNOPSIS

Throughout my career I had a continual inner battle about the proper approach to use with the boss, how to handle criticism, poor performance and employee problems, how to achieve results and what not to do in all interrelations and company activities. The Disciplined Directions Designed to prevent Disaster (the 4-D list) was designed to help guide you away from the pitfall of poor decisions or the inability to arrive at one.

The 4-D list is a magnificent reference on what not to do in the presence of the boss, your subordinates, or any of your peers. At the same time, it steers you to common sense thoughts and solutions that otherwise you would have to experience in order to learn.

I can only say that I wish I had had this list before and during my career. Finding out these things through trial-and-error is not the easiest way to go.

Don't wait for your ship to come in—
swim out to it.
—Anonymous

Never yield your courage—your courage to live,
your courage to fight, to resist, to develop
your own lives, to be free.
I'm talking about resistance to wrong
and fighting oppression.
—Roger Baldwin

19

What to Do When All Else Fails

Throughout this book, I have tried to guide, teach and motivate you to overcome adversity, build your self-confidence and reach for equality. There has been considerable direction given on identifying your problems, on recognizing your adversaries and those who discriminate against you and on identifying their methods.

I offered you a look at the past so you would be reminded of the trail of misery and unhappiness that preceded you. Your journey from near slavery to servitude to second-class acceptance weakened you. Low pay scales that kept you in a second-class status for decades, even centuries, were scrutinized and evaluated. An examination of current conditions showed only token improvements.

A challenge was put before you to set goals and prepare a path to achieve success in your career and in life. You can earn the Big One—you can be Number One. *"If it is to be—it's up to me!"* was the challenge.

"You are good," I said. Men will just have to learn to accept it. If they don't—just go around them or over them! But don't give in to them.

The two-career woman or mother's dilemma is perhaps the toughest problem you must address when you are inclined to reach for your own career. Many books and articles already written do not give you the answer. There is no one answer to these emotional problems; only spousal communication will help. There are successful examples to follow and new successes are made every day. The future will offer more help in these areas as women demand to be allowed to be as equally fulfilled as men by enjoying both a rewarding career and a family. Some companies are already providing day care, allowing you to adjust your schedules, and changing their total thinking away from the "ol' boy" theories to a more progressive approach toward women. Let's recognize these companies and thank them for their good choices and for including you in their plans.

I addressed your BEAUTY or the lack of it and hope that there is an equal amount of success out there for each of you. It isn't beauty, it's planning, hard work and self-confidence that will get you where you want to be. Achieving results is what it is all about. Self-discipline will ease the burden.

My "Learn-To-Know-What-Good-Is" theory is the basis for women to understand why success may have eluded them or to use as an advantage while just embarking upon a career. You are equal in everything—except for total acceptance by men. They just don't get it. They will if you apply the "Learn-To-Know-What-Good-Is" theory. Never before has so much been written, discussed, litigated and dramatized concerning the refusing or restricting of your rights and the suppressive treatment you have received. More and more of us realize how much we need you to help improve our standards, morals and quality of life. Look at us. We can't even come up with two outstanding candidates to run this great country. The door is wide open for you in the political arena, also.

Your *SELF-CONFIDENCE* has to be your main priority for improvement. Stop putting yourself down and telling yourself you can't do something. "I will try anything at least once," should be your motto. This approach will open your eyes to the enormous potential you have for work and success. This alone will help you live a good, rewarding and happy life.

I offered *EMPOWERMENT* by directing you toward positive thinking, toward shaking those negative feelings, remarks, cliches and choices you habitually use. Do positive things for yourself and for those around you. I promise that if you say something good about me, I will say something good about you.

ENTHUSIASM makes people strong and prevents them from dying as weaklings. Enthusiasm is the brute force *you* need to overcome the physical brute force men use. Push them around with your spirited words and lead them with your enthusiasm for success. You can do this, because now you really want to and know how to.

Both romantic love and your job have setbacks. True love just wouldn't be fun without a fight now and then. A good job isn't fun either if you don't have an occasional crisis or surprise to drive you out of your rut. Remember, the only difference between the rut and the grave is the size of the hole. Be reminded not to burden your love with the setbacks and disruptions of the job.

How do you see yourself in this maze of demands? Will you be the big winner, receiving big awards? Can you achieve the successes you want? You can—just keep telling yourself every morning how great you are. Tell yourself how superbly you did that last job—even if the boss failed to tell you. You really can measure up *if you want to.*

How about those *FOUR BOSSES* in Chapter 16 that you will have to deal with and learn to adjust to? Men are not all bad. Fact is, most are great teachers and entrepreneurs. Stay close to the good ones. Get away from the others. Don't let any of them put you down and get away with it.

To achieve what you want is a risking business; you have to keep taking big risks and avoid the ingrained habit of shunning or overreacting to risks. You can't do any of this without becoming a risk-taker or a gambler. Self-made millionaires will tell you that you can't make it big without taking a risk. If you want any measure of achievement in your life—YOU HAVE TO DO WHAT YOU HAVE TO DO.

Just in case I missed something, and to further guide you into success and out of trouble, the 4-P and 4-D Lists will help you. They are easy to follow and, while most are known to you, it's still nice to have them available as reminders for your self-improvement.

Finally, in this chapter, I have offered you a synopsis of what is already written and some advice to follow when all else fails.

It begins with reminding you again that the path to success is tough and demanding. You have to be physically and mentally prepared for the many life chapters and tests you will experience. First plan your work, then work your plan; use good common sense and be committed to yourself and to your goal. If you follow this book, you will succeed.

Should you try all of this and still can't overcome the unfair treatment that is many times the obstacle—I offer and suggest to you the use of the Civil Rights laws.

The Acts of 1964 and the Recent Civil Rights Act of 1991

These federal laws are clear and for your protection. They were written especially for women and minorities. Take advantage of them, but please don't misuse them. They will remain strong laws only if they are treated properly. Overuse kills and is self-defeating. These laws are not offered here in their entirety but only as they apply to you as a woman in the workplace. They are too encompassing to be given total treatment here. Call your local Equal Employment Opportunities Commission for additional help.

Just one more time, I would like to repeat that inspiring phrase in this book:

"We need you now—and the time is ripe."

Title VII Civil Rights Act of 1964
the E.E.O.C. Guidelines

When charges are filed by an employee alleging that an employer, employment agency, labor organization, or joint labor-management committee controlling apprenticeship or other training or retraining, including on-the-job training programs, has engaged in an unlawful employment practice, the E.E.O.C. shall serve notice of a charge against them within ten days and shall investigate the complaint. If the E.E.O.C. determines, after investigating, that there is a reasonable cause to believe the charge is true, the E.E.O.C. will hold an informal conference and attempt to use this conference plus conciliation and persuasion to eliminate the alleged unlawful practice.

The results of this informal conference are not permitted to go public and a violation means a $1000 fine or imprisonment or both.

The E.E.O.C. shall make the determination or reasonable cause A.S.A.P. and not later than 120 days from the filing date.

If the incident occurs in a state which has a state or local law prohibiting unlawful employment practice, the E.E.O.C. cannot intercede for 60 days, providing no action has been taken. A 120-day extension is possible under the state or local laws.

If within 30 days following the 120-day filing period, the E.E.O.C. has been unable to secure an acceptable agreement, the E.E.O.C. may bring civil action. If the E.E.O.C. is unable to secure an acceptable agreement, the matter then goes to the Attorney General who may bring action in the U.S. District Court.

If civil action does not result in an agreement, the aggrieved party may file civil action on her own. The court could then appoint an attorney and authorize the commencement of action with the payment of fees, costs, and security.

It is the duty of the court having jurisdiction over the proceedings to assign cases as early as possible and to expedite the case.

If the employer or any agent has in fact intentionally engaged in or is engaging in an unlawful employment practice, the court may direct the employer, etc., to stop the unlawful practice and order affirmative action, which includes reinstatement of hiring, with or without back pay. Back pay liabilities have a time limit.

Every employer, etc., is required by the law to "make and keep such records relevant to the determination of whether lawful employment practices have been or are being committed or preserve such records for such periods and make such reports therefrom as the commission shall prescribe by regulator or order. . . ."

In the Civil Rights Act of 1964, none of this applies to anyone employed by the federal government, including the military, U.S. Postal Service, and anyone employed by the District of Columbia. These are "made free from any discrimination based on race, color, religion, sex, or national origin."

Civil Rights Act of 1991

After a two-year struggle, the Civil Rights Act of 1991 was approved on November 7, 1991. It enacts a number of changes favoring alleged victims, including a "glass ceiling" commission. A provision to set up an award for diversity in American management provides, for the first time, for coverage of Senate and Presidential staffs by the major civil rights laws and requires the E.E.O.C. to carry out educational and outreach activities to establish a Technical Assistance Training Institute.

One of the new laws restores "the right of employees to challenge practices that disproportionately exclude women or minorities from America's workplace."

Section 102 of the act deals with intentional discrimination in which, prior to the act, sexual bias was not included. The new law extends compensatory and punitive damages to intentional discrimination of sex, religion and disability. Reasonable attorney fees are also provided in this new act. Back pay, interest on back pay and front pay are not included and caps do not apply to past losses such as medical bills. The cap ranges from $50K to $300K, depending on the size of the employer.

Another amendment to Title VII of the Civil Rights Act of 1964 prohibits adjusting scores, using different cutoff scores or otherwise altering results of employment-related tests on basis of race, color, religion, sex or national origin. Actual scores will have to be recorded and reported. This law also extends coverage of anti-discriminatory laws to Senate employees and political appointees of the executive branch.

The Glass Ceiling Act

Title II was added at the request of Senator Robert Dole (Rep. —Kansas). Titled "The Glass Ceiling Act of 1991," this law established a commission to study artificial barriers to the advancement of women and minorities in the workplace and to make recommendations for overcoming such barriers.

Businesses are being awarded medals for their efforts to promote the opportunities and developmental experiences of women and minorities and to encourage advancement to management and other responsible positions.

The findings by Congress included the known fact that women and minorities remain underrepresented in management and decision-making positions in business. That artificial barrier exists to prevent women and minorities from advancing.

While more women and minorities are fighting their way into the better positions, the "Glass Ceiling" is still a factor you will need to challenge as you rise in rank. Perhaps now with the government paying some attention, you will be given more consideration. The "irons are in the fire," so to speak. Now let's see how everyone complies with and plays by the rules. An important recommendation from the findings of the commission included policies and practices to fill vacancies at the management and decision-making levels with women and minorities. Developmental practices and procedures were established to ensure that these groups have access to opportunities to gain the exposure, skills and expertise necessary. The use of enforcement critical to the success of the "Glass Ceiling Act" includes a host of enforcement techniques such as litigation, complaint investigation, compliance recourse, etc. All of these are to eliminate artificial barriers. Additional studies are to be conducted as the commission deems necessary.

This Civil Rights Act of 1991 is currently in effect and can be called upon to serve your needs. This act extensively now covers those working in government and those working in the Senate who previously were governed by separate rules specifically designed for their job emphasis.

Nothing is perfect and that will include the new Civil Rights Act of 1991, but it is a furthering of your cause and helps to equalize your rights. You now have one more vehicle or tool. Don't be afraid to use it, because within the law are provisions that restrict employers from retaliation to those who choose to go to the government for assistance. Likewise, you are fully permitted to seek counsel—now at the expense of the government.

Everyone realizes that this is a tough call. It isn't easy on the mind and emotions to muster enough courage and perseverance to enter into and fight the long battle that is yours if you go to the government, and it definitely should be your last resort. Adopting this book's earlier guidance should eliminate all but the few times you will find yourself in this position. Sometimes the very threat of knowing you have the potential to seek government help will rattle enough cages to deter you from further pursuit of legal remedies. Companies and businesses do not like government people nosing around in their files. Such a process could stir up additional trouble and create serious problems for upper management. Keep this in mind if you find yourself in the awkward position of choosing between an all-out battle for recognition or standing back and giving in.

The fight is yours. It is not an easy undertaking. You did not cause women to be considered "minor" and to be treated so very poorly. If it is to stop, all women must work at it day in and day out, with each incident viewed as a challenge. Believe it or not, you are slowly winning.

One thing is certain: working hard and receiving equality in the workplace carries more than just a monetary reward—it does in fact begin to set a new, more equal social order for those who follow. That reward you must seek, and this fight you must prepare for and win.

She didn't become one of the boys,
but rather she became a catalyst of change,
one that will propel women into the new age
as leaders by choice.
—Jack McAllen

20

A Magnificent Creation: A New Prototype

Throughout this text we have illustrated the plight of women as underdogs in a man's world and we have provided them with the necessary tools, directions and encouragement to overcome adversity and move toward equality.

We have established this need for women because we know their distinct and different characteristics are necessary to cure the ills of companies and the republic. Their special gifts of nurturing, compassion, true teamwork, the ability to get to the heart of the problem and thereby attack it objectively, and their physical and mental endurance are all needed in today's workplace. When you add fairness, fair play and honesty, you quickly realize why the time is ripe for women.

These characteristics make women stronger where strength is necessary and will help them achieve their desired heights.

Single women have an advantage because they can "wing-it" and play a very flexible role. Companies and bosses like this because it offers flexibility in staff movement. However, make no mistake—while single women have an advantage, it doesn't make the climb to success that much easier.

Married women have a juggling act to perform, but they can rely on their distinctly different abilities to kick in to help achieve a win/win situation. I refer specifically to your ability to plan. It always amazes me when I see or hear of a woman who works full time, gets the kids to school (and on time), makes sure her husband gets off to work in clean clothes, finds time to help with school homework and yet finds additional time to belong to church groups or PTA or social functions.

You are better than men at detail, staying with a project until completion, making sure your completed work is accurate and acceptable and then standing ready for constructive criticism. These are attributes that make you a stronger advocate than most men. This is not a pie-in-the-sky philosophy. This is the way it is with women in the workplace. More and more aggressive women show up for work every day, ready to prove their strengths and how they use their different abilities.

It frustrates you completely when you don't know what the boss expects or you don't know what the game plan is. When you do, however, you are prepared to attack the project, work hard and fast and even set a new work pace and higher standards. Even so, you do need to continue to remind yourself that all of this takes a deep commitment and a total resolve.

Even though you know all of this, that it takes a full measure of confidence, enthusiasm, positive thinking, perseverance and a total commitment, you also know that when the playing field is level you have been accepted as an equal.

With all of this in hand you will gain greater self-confidence and in turn stronger enthusiasm toward your job and career. Now empowered, you will move toward a strong, positive attitude about yourself and about life in general. You will be ready and willing to pass on this positive stuff to your waiting associates who, as a result, will create a team of potentially strong, unbeatable players. This is the goal, the aim of every person who manages or leads people. To reach this level of competence is elating, and you will find that it is in this mode that good things happen, such as rewards, respect and the love of those around you.

Just as you are about to believe in your greatness and your new creation, you find that the job doesn't always run smoothly. Things break down; the weather isn't right; the economy takes a bad turn; there can be product problems, advertising problems, production problems and even the boss can turn on you. On the other hand, a situation of incompatibility, gender bias, stereotypical thinking or an elusive boss could be the clue that it may be time to move on. Contemporary judgment urges one to prepare to be on the move anyway, because companies are always looking for new, fresh talent and ideas. Confident women fit this qualification beautifully and are now among those being recruited to fill these needs.

You won't be surprised to find that men hold all of the power at almost every turn. You become very interested however, when you realize that you have a better reason and purpose to win that power away from them and create an entirely different work atmosphere and work ethic.

While the reference to the "good ol' boys" and their politics in this book was a real enlightenment, it was nothing compared to learning about the big role they play and the challenge they create trying to detour your quest for personal and career accomplishment. "Don't waste time with a tyrant," you were told, but do learn from those who are sincerely willing to teach and help.

Your career successes and honest recognition are the result of learning and practicing how to take risks. You also learned in this book that you had to do what was necessary to achieve success. "Whatever it takes" must become your slogan. All of the above strategies are now your key weapons needed for overcoming discrimination, rebellion and adversarial attacks.

You don't become one of the boys, but rather you become a catalyst of change, one that will propel women into the new age as leaders by choice. You will, in future time, gain more and more respect from those who once considered you a second-class human being, incapable of any real contributing strengths.

There was a defined intention herein to shake the very soul of womanhood and challenge the working woman to reject all inhuman or degrading treatment. Now, fortified with all of the tools needed to win and the encouragement and motivation to strive for success, don't be surprised when woman, this magnificent creation, raises the world to an unparalleled height of goodness and moral revival and maybe even creates a new world that would be accepted in the eyes of God.

You are now one to be reckoned with, a new and equal force, one to call on for advice and counsel; one who qualifies as an authority on decency, love and compassion; one whose track record confirms all that men really knew about but were afraid to admit and one who offers a truly different dimension to solving problems and common sense thinking.

I invite the world to shake your hand and take you at your word.

I hope we have created a new dimension for women, one that will manifest in their ability to get along with others, express their thoughts and desires and thrive on new, personal and more open relationships. Thus, by focusing on harmony and honesty, love and joy, mutual respect and meaningful communication will flourish.

Throughout this book is an emphasis on sensitivity, humanism and caring, attributes that are innate to women. These attributes are the prerequisite to correcting what is really lacking in today's workplace. I refer to the loss of loyalty from company and employee alike, loss of honest and open communication among all players, honorable give-and-take in daily negotiations and a sincere, respected camaraderie. These are elements you bring to the workplace. These will inspire a rebuilding of loyalty, trust, honesty and respect for each other

It is time once again to do business with a handshake, to be able to take a person at his word, to have companies care about and protect employees, their morale and their well being. We have had too many scrooges for too long and it's time to get back to fair play. Enter the new age woman, a catalyst arriving in the nick of time, armed with all of the good things that promote positive human experiences.

A woman will change the emphasis of work in the workplace. She will remove the exaggerated importance of the individual and dissolve the small cliques and the boardroom. This will have the effect of establishing team play in an arena where all members, big and tall, short and small, will work toward the same goal in unison, as an orchestra playing in tune at the right tempo.

Women have established themselves as a separate, distinct entity in the management ranks. They are not clones or even copies of men and do not need or want to be. The idea of women standing alone and not subject to men's business rules and philosophies is emphasized in the following paragraph, an excerpt from a remark by Barbara Grogan. The "idea" she refers to is that of not becoming a carbon copy of men in order to succeed in business.

The workplace of the future, which may or may not be distinctly female, will engage different management styles. One illustration by Mary Billard in her *Working Woman,* March 1993 article, "Do Women Make Better Managers?" is apropos. She states:

"Many say they feel relieved not to have to strain to become carbon copies of men in order to succeed in business." She goes on to cite Barbara Grogan, founder and president of Western Industrial Contractors in Denver. Mary Billard credits

Grogan's success to high levels of staff proficiency, noting, "Her strategy: flatten the corporate hierarchy and make sure that information flows freely to all staff members."

"I do not have six levels of staff," she quotes Barbara Grogan as saying, "and I don't have an organizational chart. If I did, it would be flat."

This is innovative thinking, a dramatic change and the thoughts and ideas of a pioneer, a pacesetter, an original and a revolutionary, all directed toward change in a common sense approach, a point brought forth in an earlier chapter. This new concept, that of doing things women's way, is the type of change and new thinking that will push men to change.

In their book, *Hardball for Women: Winning at the Game of Business,* published by P.G.A., 1992, Pat Heim and Susan K. Golant state, "Women are also more likely to judge and care about people based on their innate qualities rather than their position in the hierarchy."

"Because of the need to be fair, women tend to adopt a collaborative leadership style. They share information and the decision process and provide positive feedback that also ultimately helps employees grow." This is positive reformation.

Obviously, these women know the true meaning of tough management—tough-mindedness with a passion for fair play.

A New Paradigm

Those of us who have lived long enough to remember when things were more pleasant, more disciplined, more peaceful and much safer, place hope in you and in all women to reform the thinking and decisions everywhere, so future inhabitants of this great land will again enjoy law, order, common decency and opportunity at least equal to that of yesteryear, but with the inclusion of women's participation. I am sure God would wish that for us as He stands by, hoping that *you* will be the catalyst that moves and guides us to a meaningful, high quality of life, and by good example set new life styles with quality goals. Your welcomed efforts will gain enormous support along the way. Women and men are begging for quality changes. It is what everyone wants and cries out for. It can begin with one woman, you. Then, watch out and watch the changes grow.

Life on this planet is destined to change as we speed into the 21st century. Optimistically, we should hope and pray for a moral and spiritual renaissance, one that will dispel strife, hate, fear and the man-made destruction that surrounds us. When women evolve into equal alliance with men and become full participants in business based on their contributive values rather than tokenism, we may one day witness the compatibility between men and women in the workplace.

Things are rapidly changing between men and women as we witness the relaxation of competitiveness based on gender and a rise in team participation. The boss at the top will have to create projects, goals and careers in terms of results from groups, rather than results from a specific manager.

The future will see the fruition of projects completed by teams rather than goals achieved by individuals. The members of the group will be fully aware of the overall company plan, of the contribution of individual projects and of how each person contributes to the company's overall success.

Business philosophies, company attitudes and how employees view their jobs will have to change more rapidly in order to keep up with the world market. Employees will understand this and be ready and willing to react quickly and accurately. Companies can soften the extreme changes by making all employees a partner to the changes.

Since the workplace has shrunk due to downsizing, the team members will need to be cross-trained and become proficient in multiple areas. Good companies have established workshops, seminars and retraining programs to help employees through the changes.

Companies Take on a New Attitude

Women and men will find the "family-friendly" atmosphere a new but distinct part of the workplace. More and more companies will offer child care, day care provisions, father's as well as mother's leave for birth and extenuating child care and elderly care.

"The emphasis will be on productivity as companies recognize the bottom line benefits of greater productivity and reduced attrition that result from providing work and family support," as written in *Catalyst Perspective,* June 1992.

In the same article under "Company Highlights," "Companies Encourage Father's Participation," it is pointed out that men still fear loss of pay, loss of job or "that they will be considered less committed to their careers and as a result are reluctant to participate in companies where parental leave is established."

"Yet at Eastman Kodak Company, a surprisingly high number of men have taken advantage of a generous family leave policy without stigma and without derailing their careers."

One must take into account why all of this has emerged. It's women advancing and influencing the workplace that has brought about the change.

The Future

Victimized far too many times and far too long, women seeking the American Dream are seeing it dwindle before their eyes. As a result, they are forced to search for the answers, for new direction and for truth.

As we look at the bleakness of conditions today and with common-sense thinking and good conscience try desperately but unsuccessfully to find answers to all of the physical and mental turmoil and destruction, one has to be shaken by the thought that a major change is in the wind. We just can't continue destroying the beauty of the earth, each other, love for anything and everything, and then explain and excuse away the responsibility and blame for it all. Good conscience and common-sense thinking are not being permitted to work because man has set up barriers to their use.

It is going to take a great deal of the right leadership to change all of this. An enormous amount of courage, perseverance and sound judgment will be required. Maybe we should turn to God who created this magnificent earth and universe for the truth and the right direction. Right now, one must agree, proper direction and a return to good quality life is beyond the power of man alone.

In this writing, I have commissioned women to be the instigators of change. I have pushed my motivating powers to the limit to encourage them to prepare physically, mentally and spiritually to accept this limitless challenge. I feel comfortable asking them to accept this giant task of rightful leadership. I know they will succeed because of who and what they are. I asked them to get involved and take the lead because they have the good sense to seek divine help knowing that therein lies the solution. I have the courage to ask them because I have seen and witnessed their untapped display of talent and the quality decisions they are capable of making.

Let's look to the future with bright hope and elevated expectations toward the implementation in the workplace of worthwhile human and spiritual values. Some help appears to be on the way for women (and men). Could it be that we may witness improvement in family life, quality lifestyle and a moral and spiritual uplift?

Maybe we will experience men and women respecting each other for who they are as a basis for genuine relationships, the family united rather than fragmented or even destroyed, and all willing to face and accept their individual responsibilities without fear and frustration of constant setback or defeat.

You know, maybe we will also see men and women dancing together instead of apart. And maybe we may once again see sex practiced only after marriage, resulting in true love, respect and real happiness. It could even be that God's name will be spoken again with respect and adoration by this better-educated, clearer-thinking society. I pledge to you, it is worth the effort.

Total Quality Management

The workplace will change also as companies begin to focus on results rather than quotas. Companies are beginning to survey their employees, asking questions about their needs to carry out their job functions more productively and what tools or new aids would improve their performance. The results coming in are astounding and clearly indicate that everyone is now focusing on what is going right in their work and building on that new approach.

Women will benefit from this new approach because, in theory, employees are expected to manage their own jobs. This will enable all women to progress as a result of their efforts. In addition this new philosophy creates a work-together ethic where employees (including women) can open up and help solve problems and work toward common goals. This creates a spiritual investment in the success of each other and the company.

The end result so far has been quite clear: companies have unwittingly instituted a total-quality program, one which has no gender or discriminating flaws. Quality is what the customer is after. It pushes leaders to foster joy in work, harmony and teamwork. It is in this setting that women can thrive as women and make use of their feminine traits. It is in this setting that bosses type C and D will bite the dust.

Thanks for the great time we shared. Now take my hand and lead the way. Show how *you* are going to manage your way to the top. It will be a real pleasure going to work each day when *The Boss Is a Woman.*

The signals of the century proclaim the things that
are to be, the rise of woman to her place,
the coming of a nobler race.
—Angela Morgan

Bibliography

BOOKS

Dearest Amanda—An Executive's Advice to Her Daughter.
Eliza Collins, Harper and Row, 1984.

The Managerial Woman
Margaret Hennig and Anne Jardin, Anchor Press/Doubleday, 1977.

Women Who Want to Be Boss
Marlene Jensen, Doubleday and Co., Inc., 1987.

Women Executives in a Changing Environment
Margaret Fenn, Prentice Hall, 1980.

The Working Woman Report
Editions of Working Women with Gay Bryant, Simon and Schuster, 1984.

The New Entrepreneurs
Terri P. Tepper and Nona Dawe Tepper, Jean Ray Laury, Universe Books, 1980.

Breaking the Glass Ceiling
Ann Morrison, Addison-Wesley Publishing, 1987.

American Working Woman
Rosalyn Boxandall, Linda Gordon, Susan Reverby, Random House.

The Quiet Rebel
Glynis M. Breakwall, Grove Press, 1986.

Successful Women/Angry Man
Bebe Moore Campbell, Jove Books, 1986.

Success and Betrayal: The Crisis of Women in Corporate America
Nehana Jacobs, Touchtone Books—Simon and Schuster, 1986.

The Best of Friends, The Worst of Enemies
Eva Margolis, Doubleday, 1985.

An Attitude From Power Failure
Barbara Buals, Lydia Swan, St. Martins Press, 1989.

Hardball for Women: Winning at the Game of Business
Pat Heim and Susan K. Golant, AGA Publishing Group, 1992.

Points: The Most Practical Program Ever *to Improve Your Self-Image*
David A. Gustafson, Blue Dolphin Publishing, 1992.

The Quotable Woman
Elaine Partinow, Corwin Books, 1977.

Contemporary Quotes
James B. Simpson, Vali-Bollow Press, 1964.

Good Advice
William Saffire and Leonard Safir, Timebooks, 1982.

The Morrow Book of Quotations in American History
Josphe R. Conlin, New York: Morrow, 1984.

MAGAZINES

Business Month Magazine, "Men vs. Women," Glenda Blair, Oct. 1990.

Essence Magazine, "Take Charge," Judy D. Simmons, Oct. 1988.

Glamour, "You're Underpaid Yet You Don't Complain," Marilyn Moats Kennedy, Nov. 1988.

Savvy Woman, "Fashion Victims (Women Executives in Retailing)," June 1990.

Working Woman, "A Secret Formula for Success," Kathleen Fury, Nov. 1988.

Working Woman, "The Fine Art of Getting Your Boss to Change," Mardell Grothe and Peter Wylie.

LECTURE

Revised Version, 1987 Cheryl Miller Lecture, "Sexual Differential and the Devaluation of Women's Work," Barbara F. Reskin.